PREPARATION TOOLS FOR SINGLES & PRESERVATION FOR COUPLES

EDUCATIONAL/INPIRATIONAL

ANGELA C. GRIFFITHS

Unless otherwise indicated, all scripture quotations are taken from the King James Version of the Bible.

1st Printing

Preparation Tools for Singles & Preservation for Couples

ISBN 9798344208343

Copyright ©2024 by Angela C. Griffiths

Published by

Angela C. Griffiths

Printed in the United States of America. All rights reserved under International Copyright Law. This book or parts thereof may not be reproduced in any form, stored in a retrieval system, or transmitted in any form by any means- electronic, mechanical, photocopy, recording, or otherwise- without prior written permission of the publisher, except as provided by United States of America copyright law.

Dedications

First, I give all honor, glory, and praise to the Lord, who inspired me to write these words and placed them in my heart and spirit for this book.

This book is dedicated to my beloved parents, Nashford and Inez Griffiths. Their lives, love, integrity, humility, and peaceful ways toward others have left an indelible mark on me. They instilled in me the confidence to walk in their footsteps, follow God, and always strive to do good.

To my daughter, Nicole, who has stood by me, loving me unconditionally through all circumstances—I am forever grateful.

Acknowledgements

To the late Pastor, **Dr Zachery Tims Jr.** The visionary of N.D.C.C. I acknowledge him with permission and would like to express my sincere appreciation, he was instrumental to me in and through his teachings, he taught me to push and pursue after my God given purpose and destiny.

To Apostle Nathaniel & First Lady Washington, pastors who was instrumental to me through their teachings, I would like to express my sincere appreciation to both of you, and I will never forget your help and encouragement through the trying times.

Special Thanks

Darlene, Joshua, Christine, Anna, Calvin, Princess, Renae, Stephanie, and the many others who were there for me.

Epigraph

"The search for that soulmate for life & Preserving the relationship once they are found"

TABLE OF CONTENTS

Chapter 1
Your Love Relationship.. 1

Chapter 2
A Need for Companionship and Relationship................... 11

Chapter 3
Characteristics and Traits to Seek in A Relationship 15

Chapter 4
Time is the Waiting Game 32

Chapter 5
Equally Yoke Relationships for Singles.............................40

Chapter 6
Unequally Yoke Relationships for Singles 44

Chapter 7
Singles with Children 52

Chapter 8
Age! Does It or Does Not Matter....................................... 54

Chapter 9
Singles Caught Up Into the Dating Limbo 61

Chapter 10
Celebrating Special Occasions During Courtship 66

Chapter 11
Disagreements During Courtship 68

Chapter 12
Do Not Cry It Is Far Your Good 71

Chapter 13
Always Be Number One 74

Chapter 14
The Transitional Phase 76

Chapter 15
Preservation for Couples & The Marriage Relationship ... 81

Chapter 16
Married But Feels Single 90

Chapter 17
Spending Quality Time With God 101

Chapter 18
Forgiveness In Marriages 104

Chapter 19
Healthy Habits and Lifestyles for Married Couples 112

Chapter 20
Scripture References for Couples 114

Chapter 21
Married Couples In An Unequally Yoke Relationship ... 123

Chapter 22
Turning Your House Into a Home 127

Chapter 23
Couples Celebrating Special Occasions 134

Chapter 24
Sexual Manipulations In Marriages 137

Chapter 25
Disagreements In Marriages 141

Chapter 26
Authority Figures In Marriages 144

Chapter 27
Pride- Disrespect and Abuse In Marriages 147

Chapter 28
To The Widows and Widowers 150

Chapter 29
Continuing the Romance 152

Introduction

This book was written to help singles and couples from all walks of life, including Christians and non-Christians. It will inspire, encourage, and motivate you to pursue a long-lasting, better relationship during courting and marriage.

This will guide our singles to know what they want and what to look for in a relationship so that they can make an appropriate decision when choosing a mate. Meanwhile, married couples will get useful tools to help with the do's and don'ts and help preserve their marriages.

Special Dedicated Prayers to All Singles

This Is a Personal Prayer of Encouragement and Strength While You Wait.

To all my dedicated single readers, with you in mind as I wrote this book the Lord gave me this prayer for you while you wait for your "Boas & Ruth".

Lord teaches me patience to wait, and to walk when you want me to walk, teach me to run when you want me to run, guide my thoughts, my heart, my words, guide and direct my paths, to be able to see spiritually, and to know spiritually who to connect with to give my heart and to love. Teach me to have that vertical one on one relationship with you first in all areas of my life and help me to find and fall in love with my first true love which is you! then help guide me to that human love that will compliment me, but only you can and will complete me.

CHAPTER 1
YOUR LOVE RELATIONSHIP

"For church singles who never thought of getting involved in activities they dreamed of doing but never had the time to pursue or learn, now is the time."

Now, as you can see, you do not need to be sad because you do not have a friend or a special someone to go out with. I am not saying it is not nice to have someone you can share and do things with, but as a single you need to continue being independent, depend only on the Lord to help you establish yourself in making your own money, car, home and business, many single people do better in life than some couples.

As a single person if you have not found that special person and do not know your calling or purpose in life you will first need to consult God for direction and find out what it is that you should be doing for the kingdom of God, once you find out what it is you will now have a purpose for living. Most people's misconception is once they have found that mate they think they will be complete and totally happy, this is not true, having companionship does help, but what if that relationship fails, then what? the only true love you can truly fall back on is God, no matter what situation you may find yourself in, he says "I will never leave you nor forsake you". Hebrews13vs5. When men leave you, God will always be there, so singles as your search continues, for that true love, that individual you seek to be your soul mate, let us reflect back on that word.

"True love" God is your number one true love, you must first love him before you can love others, Him first then yourself, then others, because if you do not love yourself then how can you give something you do not have!

Though our parents love us, some would not give up their lives for their children, how about their friends or strangers? no matter how good or generous they are would they? would you?

Even when you are unlovable, unroyal, ungrateful, towards him for years because of his loving mercy and grace he continues to love you. This one-sided love is known as un reciprocal but he being patiently waits on you just because he loves you. As humans we require shared love, it is when two people equally share and give their love to each other.

God is faithful to you more that any man or woman will or could ever give you. He will never cheat on you, lie to you, hurt you, or hate you because you make some mistakes, or his love starts to fade away because he is tired of you, or because you are getting older and there are changes in your life. If you do not know that kind of love, I dare you to try him first.

Preparations Before Starting A Relationship

Before you start or enter any relationship it is very important that before you decide to take the dive you must be prepared, there are different stages of preparation. I would like you to look at this example.

I will start by using this analogy of a woman who wants to have a baby, to show you just as in any relationships it is just as important one must be ready, or it could fail. That woman's body must be prepared and ready to carry a baby to full term, her body must be ready physically, mentally and emotionally stable for pregnancy. But first there are the physical aspects. If a woman has not conditioned her body for the proper nutrition to eat healthy foods in advance, months prior to pregnancy that baby's health and life may be compromised, her life is at risk too and that baby may born with all kinds of problems, such as low birth weight, and other abnormalities depending on the severity of the malnutrition, especially if this woman is a smoker or if she on drugs and do not try to stop or else the baby during are after birth may be born with severe respiratory problems, and other severe abnormalities, withdrawals or death. Second, she must be Mentally/Emotionally prepared to handle the responsibilities of a baby, changing, feeding, sickness, up at nights, crying, and the financial responsibilities for the next 18 to 20 years and the different stages of growth.

Starting A Relationship

In the event you have decided to start or get involved in any relationships, it is a must, you need to be prepared and ready for the next step. You need to be prepared spiritually, spiritually you are being lined up where God wants you to be, he is working on you and in you making changes and fine tuning you, he is also working on the person he is preparing for you, you will be able to discern certain things in a person, and about a person, he will connect you with that person who are in close or equal spiritual alignment as you, they will be on fire as you, they will love to praise and worship like you and things around you.

Mentally he is preparing you by changing your thinking, your mind set from some selfish behaviors you may have developed during your years of being single.

Emotionally, you need to be stable, balanced and can take the ups and downs in stressful life situations and be strong to bounce back regardless of what comes your way. First thing you must do is to pray and ask God for spiritual guidance and physical direction. You need to ask for patience to wait for the right person He has for you, while you wait stay focus on the things he wants and called you to do, stay busy so you will not get distracted and lose your focus, if you do not ask and wait patiently, you in your "natural fleshly side" will tend to rise up and see what you want to see with the "natural eyes" and run after it because you desire to have it just because it looks good from the outside. pray specifically for what you desire in that person, and make sure it is one who is "equally yoke" and one that is compatible with you, make sure they are bearing "Godly fruits as the word says" and their words are followed by their actions. Make sure they have class and integrity.

Know your likes and dislikes, ask specific questions. Singles, know that God wants the best for you, he wants you whole, he wants you to be blessed, happy and to be treated with love and respect, not verbal, physical, mental or sexual abuse this is why it is very imperative you take your time and wait on him, if not examine all aspects of the individual you are dating give it time to see what God wants you to see in each individuals before you commit. Do not base your relationship off emotions or outer appearance only, but again wait on the holy spirit to guide you, he will give you that gut feeling (unction in your guts) that something is not right, follow that, do not doubt.

Many singles, both males and females look forward to that day when the Lord will send and bless them with that special someone and if it comes it is wonderful, if not do not get depressed, discouraged, because I believed God wants us to be happy with another human companionship it
is possible it is not the right time. As the cliché goes "God may not come when you want him, but he is always on time".

As a single being alone does not mean you are dead and the world stops, while you are waiting you need to find friends, that means you will find things you enjoy doing that make you happy, other than a job. If you have no friends be happy in the Lord, enjoy your success in life and do things by yourself, pamper and treat yourself to the fine things life has to offer, go to the movies, go out to a concerts or plays, or go watch live games such as basketball, football, baseball, go skating or bike riding, treat yourself to dinner, go shopping, go to the beach, go to the park and bring a book to read that is appealing to you, go and get a massage and a manicure and pedicure, now do you see how many things you could do that you may not though about, how about singles activities at your church! for singles that you never thought of getting involved in activities you dreamed of doing but never had the time to do them or learn how, now is the time.

It's getting worse. As we get closer to the end. Of time. That is. The end times. As the scripture spoke about. It speaks. In the book of First Peter 4:17, For it is time for judgment to begin with God's household; and if it begins with us, what will the outcome be for those who do not obey the gospel of God?

Some of our churches nowadays are like a fashion show or a form of. Christian. Club Party except the alcohol and never mind. Some do go home. To the alcohol. Not justifying or putting anyone down. Who is weak? And. Are still being healed. By the Lord from this illness. But this is what some of our churches are coming to. That's the reason. The time is. Being. Shortened. Speeding up? And the Bible is. Being fulfilled. Too many. Hypocrites. Liars. Backstabbers. Haters and boasters. Nevertheless. The few real. People. And genuine people that are called and are not straddling the fence.

Now, as you can see, you do not need to be sad because you do not have a friend or a special someone to go out with. I am not saying it is not nice to have someone you can share and do things with, but as a single you need to continue being independent, depend only on the Lord to help you establish yourself in making your own money, car, home and business, many single people do better in life than some couples.

Your Love Relationship

As a single person if you have not found that special person and do not know your calling or purpose in life you will first need to consult God for direction and find out what it is that you should be doing for the kingdom of God, once you find out what it is you will now have a purpose for living. Most people's misconception is once they have found that mate they think they will be complete and totally happy, this is not true, having companionship does help, but what if that relationship fails, then what? the only true love you can truly fall back on is God, no matter what situation you may find yourself in, he says "I will never leave you nor forsake you". Hebrews13vs5. When men leave you, God will always be there, so singles as your search continues, for that true love, that individual you seek to be your soul mate, let us reflect on that word.

"True love" God is your number one true love, you must first love him before you can love others, Him first then yourself, then others, because if you do not love yourself then how can you give something you do not have!

Though our parents love us, some would not give up their lives for their children, how about their friends or strangers? no matter how good or generous they are would they? would you?

Even when you are unlovable, unroyal, ungrateful, towards him for years because of his loving mercy and grace he continues to love you. This one-sided love is known as un-reciprocal, but he patiently waits on you just because he loves you. As humans we require shared love, it is when two people equally share and give their love to each other. God is faithful to you more that any man or woman will or could ever give you. He will never cheat on you, lie to you, hurt you, or hate you because you make some mistakes, or his love starts to fade away because he is tired of you, or because you are getting older and there are changes in your life. If you do not know that kind of love, I dare you to try him first.

CHAPTER 2
A NEED FOR COMPANIONSHIP & RELATIONSHIP

Because God is love, He made you and I to have a need and desires to be loved a need to love others and share one's life with another. So, this is why you as an individual, we as people crave the need to be loved and being in a relationship, being in and or falling in love with someone not just any relationship but a true and healthy one, one that is conducive to mutual open communication, trust, honesty, commitment, respect and integrity.

But in order for God to truly bless you, you must understand that you need to do some things in order to be blessed such as soul searching, it will not hurt letting go of some baggage's of the past in order to move on to a bright future, but you and only you knows what these things are that you need to let go of. Such as past hurts, pains, unforgiveness and guilt that will hold you captive as prisoners from past relationships.

I have been there. I know it is hard at times to move forward some time when you think you have totally let go our minds are like a recorder that rewind and replays over and over again past situations the enemy will plant in your thoughts. These are known as familiar spirits, they are usually triggered by past situation and circumstances, these are spirits that brings back memories of the past of something or someone or places by the way of using that thing to trigger your memories of something familiar, when you think you are over it, it sneaks up on you and haunts you again, these are things will harm you and keep you stagnant. Past situations such as divorce, abusive relationships, psychological triggers, that triggers your emotional reactions, old habits, such as smoking, drinking, sex, drugs, partying, gambling, loss of an employment, loss of a home sickness, depression, anger, stressors of life and past failures, but you must be strong, you can do it by canceling those thoughts through the word and focus them on things that are more positive, things that will excel you forward, focus on things positive that will keep you busy.

Spirits That Keep You from Moving Forward

Familiar Spirits

These are some of the four major things the enemy uses to keep you bound. Situations, places, things and people. These are the things the devil uses to remind you of your past, you may have one or more of these situations, that is why they are called "familiar spirits"

Let me give you some examples, you may have been in a relationship in the past, that relationship has been ended years ago and one day all of a sudden as you were minding your business on your way home, your ex suddenly just pops up in your though, and you starts to reminisce on the past what if that relationship worked out where would you be now or what could have been, the times spend together, and wondering what they are doing now! or you may have seen someone who resembles your ex. or certain smells such as perfumes, colognes, foods, personalities, laughs, talks, walks, shapes may trigger memories of the past. It could be places you have been to such as restaurants, a house that resembles one you may have lived in the past. It could be a situation you have been in at the present and it triggers something from the past they call it like DeJa'Vu, and it is happening all over again.

Soul Ties

This is another area of baggage's we carry around that keeps us bound and keeps you from moving forward into some relationships that are ordained by God, these are spirits that keeps you bound and tied to another person from the past even though that relationship has been severed, and resolved for years this tie is usually through sex, sexual intimacy with someone from your past, it is a spiritual soul ties connection, that ties you and keep pulling and drawing you back to them, though that relationship is not the best for you, it keeps you going back because of the sexual ties between both individuals though you are in another relationship or tries to move on into another relationship to break free.

CHAPTER 3
CHARACTERISTICS AND TRAITS TO SEEK IN A RELATIONSHIPS

It is vital when you are seeking a relationship to look for certain traits in a person, one of the best guides is from the scriptures, It will guide you into these area's we tend to overlook many times, this is your guidebook and map that will never steer you wrong.

At this stage in a relationship these are some of the fruit or traits you should be striving for these are called the "Fruit of The Spirit".

The first is: Love, the second is: Joy, the third is: Peace, the fourth is: Gentleness, the fifth is: Goodness, the sixth is: Faith, the seventh is: Meekness, the eighth is: Temperance and ninth is: Long suffering. This is from Galatians 5 verses 19-23.

If you do not see at least five or more of these as a spiritual guide and are at least working towards the rest this should be a "red flag" watch and be cautious, in addition to the other traits trust, effective communication skills and honesty these are just a few very important information you need to look for, test them and see if they are selfish, ask hard questions, make up situational questions to ask listen and examine their answers carefully especially if you are interested and want to move forward and continue to pursing courting, watch for their actions, their behavior. Sometimes people will give you some correct answers, answers they know you want to hear but their actions speak louder than words and this is because a person can only "act" for so long until they are exposed. Ask if he or she is committed to t w long have they been a Christian? how are they doing in their spiritual walk with Christ? how often do they attend church and bible study? Do not forget to be discreet and check out their mannerisms.

These Ae Some of The Traits Single Men Need To Look for In a Woman:

A God Fairing Woman

A Woman Who Is Faithful

A Committed and Loyal Woman

A Woman with Integrity

A Woman with Humility

An Honest Woman

A Trustworthy Woman

A Respectful Woman

A Woman Who Is Family Oriented

A Woman Who Is Kind

A Woman, Who Is Not Lazy She, Is A Help Mate

A Woman Strong Woman

A Good Communicator

A Woman Who Is Romantic & Intimate and has a high sex drive

Remember no one is perfect, but they should have at least half of these traits and are striving to improve in the area's they are lacking in.

These Are Some of The Traits A Single Women Need to Look for In a Man:

A God Fairing Man

A Man Who Is Honest

A Man Who Is Trustworthy

A Man Who Is Faithful

A Man Who Is a Provider

A Man Who Is Loyal

A Man Who Is Committed

A Man Who Has Good Communication Skills

A Man Who Is a Good Listener

A Family Man

A Man with Leadership Qualities

A Man Who Is Respectful

A Man Who Is Strong

A Man Who Is Romantic & Intimate

A Man Who likes to be Intimate

A Man with Humility

A Kind Man

A Man with Integrity

Remember no one is perfect, but they should have at least half of these traits and are striving to improve in the area's they are lacking in.

Ask about something you need clarity about, know this once you get into hard times in your relationship some of those same people who pushed you into making a quick decision you will not find when trouble comes.

Women Know Your Man. Know what you want in a man but know what to look for in a man.

Women you need to know your man. As singles, if you are in a committed long-term relationship that will eventually leads into marriage, it is absolutely vital to learn and know as much as possible about the character of this individual you are planning to spend the rest of your life with knowing your man before you make a permanent, long term decision, although you may have gotten engaged or already set a wedding date, if you are unsure and need more time just to make sure you do so, do not let anyone rush or push them when you need them, so find out more and take your time. After all you are only planning to spend the rest of your life with this individual.

First make sure the relationship is "Ordained by God" make sure he is that "Boas" God send for you, not a "Boo or Bozo". Most important seek after a God-Fearing Man one that really loves the Lord, not one that is lake warm, and is straddling the fence, one that speaks and does what he says by his actions, if this man loves the Lord, he will love you as he loves himself and treat you as the queen you are, as the bible states.

Seek after one that is Faithful, because if he is faithful to God he will also be faithful to you, even with your imperfections. Look for a man with Integrity, is one who is honest, sincere and is upright in what he does, he has sound moral principles and judgments.

The definition says it all about this man, who would not want this in a man, sisters as you already know it is hard to find a good man like this in these days but be encouraged God still have a few of these jewels hidden just for you.

Seek after a Loyal and Committed Man, this kind of man will be loyal to the relationship and he will be committed to you and taking care of his responsibilities, and when hard times come, he will not run away or fall apart.

Seek after a Strong Man, this is one who is strong spiritually and mentally, when it gets rough during hard times, he will be there for you, he will not have abandoned you during times of trouble.

Women, seek after a man who is a Provider, this is one who can provide for you and his family, one who is not lazy, God made him the head to provide for his home, men, our women number one need in a relationship is security, even though at times in this society we feel very

independent as women we need a man who is a provider, and you are his help mate.

Women you need to seek after men that are Leaders or those with Leadership qualities one who know how to take care of business, he will take care of his responsibilities.

A Family Oriented Man is one who usually has a close relationship with his family, this is a man who will most likely wants his own family in the future he will love a care for them.

As women, we need a man that is a good listener and communicator, one who is willing to talk and listen regardless, one who is willing to improve on these skills if he is lacking in this area, this is a critical part of your relationship, it is for understanding, this could make or break your relationship and this is where most men retreat, if you have good communication in your relationship it will usually have a good chance to last.

Next seek after a Honesty, a honest man will respect you enough to tell you the truth even if it hurts, he will not cheat steal or lie to you, he is trust worthy, fair, sincere and straight forward with you.

Sisters seek after one who is Respectful in his mannerism towards you, he will not insult and embarrassed you in public places, family or friends, he will be able to control his behavior until the appropriate time and place, he will hold you in high regards, he has a good attitude towards you and others.

Seek a man who is Kind he will not be stingy, he will not hold "things" in high regards as if it is too good for you, he will be a giver.

Finally seek after one who is Romantic, a man who is romantic usually aim to please, he acknowledges special occasions, he does small things that catches her attention, he gives her accolades and compliments, he surprises her, just because! he is spontaneous, a woman likes to get out and like to be wine and dine, dinners, movies and shopping, take short walks on the beach, picnics and hobbies.

Women, seek after a man who is Trustworthy, you can trust him with just about anything.

Seek after a man who is Intimate, not only in love making, but you will be able to be transparent with each other, free and open to be yourself around him.

Men Know Your Woman. Know what you want in a woman but know what to look for in a woman.

As single men it is important to know your woman and what it is that you are looking for in that woman you are planning to give your heart to. My brothers, if you are truly seeking a long term committed relationship that will eventually leads to marriage, that soul mate you will share the future with, again it is crucial that you know for sure she is that special diamond, she is that "Ruth" the one who is Ordained by God for you.

Men I know you tend to have a eye for women with a beautiful figure and a pretty face, but do not end up with a

Delilah and pure heart aches, nothing is wrong with having the complete package and a God faring woman, but you must ask and wait on the Lord.

Men there is nothing better than seeking after a God-Fearing Woman, she is one who loves the Lord with all her heart and mind, she follows the precepts of the word as the bible states. She will value her vows, honor, love and respect you.

Seek a woman with Integrity, she is a woman of class, she is mindful of how and what she does, she is one who respects herself, she is intelligent and intellectual, she is goal focused and oriented, she is sincere and honest, she has sound moral principles and judgments.

Next seek after one who is Faithful, if she is faithful to God in all her ways, she will be faithful and trustworthy to you also.

Seek after a Humble woman, one that is not prideful and laid back, she is not the boastful type because she knows who make it all possible.

Also, you need to seek after a Loyal and Committed Woman, she is trustworthy, you can trust her in what she says or does, she will be committed to you only even if you do not do your part, do your part men.

Seek after a Strong Woman one who is strong spiritually and mentally, she will be able to overcome hard times, stressful situations and troubled times without falling apart.

Seek after a Honest Woman she has good morals, she will not cheat or steal from you and others, she has good Judgments, she is trustworthy and straight forward and gets to the point.

Continue and seek after a Respectful Woman, this kind will love, respect and cherish you for who you are, she will treat you like the "king" that you are in her eyes, she will look up to you with high esteem and regards. She will not disrespect or embarrass you in public places and is able to have self-control until the appropriate time.

Seek after a woman that who is a good Communicator, this woman tends to have good communication skills and follow through with her commitments by prioritizing and knowing that communication is the key to a long-lasting relationship and keeping everything in check.

A Woman with Family Oriented Background, this woman is family minded, she is usually closely knit with her family, she is the kind of woman that will be able to keep a home together, she is one who takes her responsibilities seriously and one who will take care of her husband and children.

Seek a woman who is Kind, she will give or do almost anything for you, nothing will be too good for you, she will give you, her heart.

Seek after a woman that is not Lazy do not mind working, she is your help mate.

Seek a woman who is Romantic, when I speak about romance, I am not talking only sexually, because we as women knows men loves sex, she will "woo" you, she will pay close attention to you on special and non-special occasions, she will acknowledge you by giving you compliments and accolades.

Seek after a Trustworthy woman, she will not deceive you, she will love you for who you are.

Seek after an Intimate woman, she will be transparent with herself and you, she will be able to be herself around you and you around her. She is the kind of woman that is not afraid to make love.

Relationships Ordained By God

I know you are probably asking the question. How do I know when my relationship is ordained by God, or How will I know when an individual is ordained for me?

First, God is not the author of confusion, when he does things, he does them decent and in order, you will have peace in your spirit, and you will know in your spirit confirmed by the spirit.

When God ordained a relationship, he will bring the two people together, He will always speak to each individual so both will know before they are brought together, or he will show each individual their mate in either dreams or visions and then confirm it and then connection them together somehow, so they can meet, once they have met, no matter what weaknesses or faults they may have they will complement each other, once they enter into a relationship, no matter what storms of life may arise they will be able to with stand and overcome any problems or storms and your relationship will last until death do you apart.

Perfect Scripture Reference To Follow For The Traits

You Seek In Your Soulmate

This is one of the best references to follow as single individuals when seeking your mate

seek after a PROVERB 31vs 10- 31 for women and men.

Who is a virtuous woman? She is one who has no value of money or things cannot buy her, her love cannot be bought because of her integrity.

VS10. "Who can find a virtuous woman? for her price is far above rubies.

The heart of her husband doth safely trust in her, so that he has no need of spoil.

She will do him good and not evil all the days of his life.

She seeketh wool, and flax, and worketh willingly with her hands.

She is like the merchant's ship; she bringeth her food from afar.

She riseth also while it is yet night, and giveth meat to her household, and a portion to her maidens.

She considereth a field and buyeth it: with the fruit of her hands, she planteth a vineyard.

She girdeth her loins with strength, and strengtheneth her arms.

She perceiveth that her merchandise is good: her candle goeth not out by night.

She layeth her hands to the spindle, and her hands, yea, she reacheth forth her hands to the needy.

She is not afraid of the snow for her household: for all her household is clothed with scarlet.

She maketh herself coverings of tapestry; her clothing is silk and purple.

Her husband is known in the gates, when he sitteth among the elders of the land.

She maketh fine linen, and selleth it; and dilivereth girdles unto the merchant.

Strength and honour are her clothing; and she shall rejoice in the time to come.

She openeth her mouth with wisdom; and in her tongue is the law of kindness.

She looketh well to the ways of her household, and eateth not the bread of idleness.

Her children rise and call her blessed; her husband also, and he praiseth her.

CHAPTER 4
TIME IS THE WAITING GAME

Now that you have examined the traits to know what to look for in an individual, this is the hard part for most people, this is considered to be the waiting period.

As newly courting or dating couples, timing is very important, you must be very patient to wait during this time.

As time passes by, you will be able to see and get to know the "real" person you are with, it only takes time to reveal all things. With time on your side, you will see the good and the bad in a person, and eventually the "true character" will surface. Timing will also make or break a relationship, again timing is key to unlock all hidden treasures, either bad or good.

With time, you must give your relationship, the winter, spring, summer and fall season, a complete season to test, examine, and evaluate each other. A 365 day to get out the "butterflies" the "sweet girl" or the "nice guy" syndrome, until you can prove otherwise. Again, people can act for so long until the truth is revealed.

Your Complete Seasons

Winter, Spring, Summer, Fall is consisted of four cycles. As a newly courting and dating couple, you both need to take the time and wait to test each cycle.

Winter Cycle

In the winter, it represents "cold" harsh weather conditions in our natural world of nature. This is the same with your relationship, some days are cold, harsh and windy, some days are milder than others old with no wind, some days are warmer with sunshine, some are cold and rainy with no sunshine and others days are cold, rainy, windy with no sunshine and on other days you may have cold, rain and hail that causes everything to freeze when the temperature drops lower and it becomes unbearable because of the changes, but at this time each person must adjust or reevaluate themselves for these changes that occurs in life, because things do not stay the same every day, each person must find the best way to keep warm in order to survive.

Spring Cycle

As you know spring is right after winter, the weather fluctuates sometimes from cold, cool to warm, sometimes it is windy and at times calm, sometimes it is cloudy followed by rain and at times sunny or a combination of both.

But the majority of the time spring brings rain, this cycle is a time for new growth, birth and new life cycle. It is a new beginning, a fresh start for the plants that blossom and bloom, a refreshing change from the harsh winter to regrowth from the cold and animals and birds to come out from hibernation that brings new life.

Summer Cycle

From the calm comfortable temperature of spring and the newness of life and freshness in the air from the plants, push summer in its fullness, the days are mostly sunny hardly any rain, as it arrives it replenishes and beautifies and sometime the temperature sores too high it is too hot and it becomes over whelming and uncomfortable, followed by high humidity, but longer days to enjoy the sunshine and nature.

Fall Cycle

Now after the summer ends the fall begins, temperature changes again from the hot humid summer to a cooler more comfortable one, the leaves on the trees start to change colors and sheds, the animals prepare for hibernation again, the evening become shorter, and at

times the temp drops low as it gets closer to the winter you must once again adjust to the climate changes and accommodate the new change in the season once again. This is also the same with life changes, you must learn to accommodate these changes in life too. Some days will be hot, some days cold, some days with harsh conditions such as hail, some days cool and breezy, some day's rain, and on another day's calm with clear skies, perfect temperature and sunshine all day.

Signs For Red Flags

Now, these are some of the signs and behaviors to look for in your relationships before you decide to continue courting or dating, or before you accept a proposal of marriage. Now just as there is good there is bad also, and you need to know and observe these very close therefore it is very important to take your time and give it the "Complete Season" to see these traits emerging. This is why it is important to pray first and ask God to reveal things about an individual, sometimes is take just days and things starts to surface. If you are a Christian sister or brother do not be surprised if you see some of these traits surfaces, you must remember no one is perfect, and God is still working on a lot of us, and therefore we have the church, it is a "Hospital" for the spiritually sick people and for mentally, emotionally and physical needy.

There are all kinds of circumstances that leads up to some of these issues, you also must recognize when they were in the world these habits developed or again those generation curses followed them that have not been broken and some are still immature in their walk.

Verbal Abuse

This involved verbally attacking you by cursing, disrespectful towards you, talking down, belittling, taunting, teasing.

This involved physically fighting, hitting or slapping, pinching, punching, torturing such as burning, scratching, cutting, slashing, squeezing as in choking, spitting and biting, pulling as by an arm, hair, nose, ears and bending or Twisting a body part such as fingers and arms.

Obsessive Behaviors

These are individuals who go beyond controlling and possessive, these are extreme in their habits and behaviors, they will not take no for an answer, they do not like rejections, these are usually your stalkers, they will watch, follow and torment you everywhere you go, they will tend to approach and force you to do things against your will, and if you resist they will get angry and become extremely physical towards you.

For example, if you are in a relationship with a individual like this he or she won't take no for an answer, they hate being rejected, if you decides to end the relationship you may experience the following, verbal and physical abuse, stalking, torments and threats, such as forcing you to stay with them and if you do not they will verbally warn you and may say something like this, If I cannot have you no one else will. Individuals like these will kill.

Other Red Flags Behaviors to Observe

If you are friends leading into a relationship, and one of the individuals in that friendship constantly making promises and makes excuses for breaking these promises, stop! do not go any further into a relationship with this individual, they are already starting off wrong by making excuses and telling lies, you must first start a relationship with trust.

If you are friends leading into a relationship, and you notice they are being persistent, in trying to invite you to their home, or they are trying to invite themselves to your home either night or day. Stop! and kick them to the curb and drop them like a bad habit. This is what I called " a pimp" he or she is trying to get you into bed, these people only have one thing on their mind, sex, and if you are weak, they will get you because they know you are single and the flesh gets weak at times, you are their prey and they will prey on you until they get what they want and dump you for their next victim.

If you notice an individual is perusing after you, acknowledging your every presence, giving you compliments, greeting you. But not quite verbalizing and you attempt to know more information about them by asking specific questions and they will not answer, or they say they will get back to you and never did. Take it that they are possibly involved and are lying and have no communication skills. Do not waste your time thinking that there is a chance of a relationship you would only be setting up yourself to get hurt ,move on, do not be a escape goat for anyone guard your heart at all cost.

Motives

Check out a person motives when they are doing something for you, check if it is truly from the heart or if they are doing it for some other reason.

CHAPTER 5
EQUALLY YOKE RELATIONSHIPS FOR SINGLES

Single sisters and brothers. Do you know you are God's leading men and women; you are leaders, and He wants you to seek leaders or leadership qualities like yourselves to uplift, encouraged and complement each other, He do not want you to settle for less than the best, or sell yourself cheap! Sisters you are a "Diamond in the Making" even though you may be under some pressure right now, you are in the process of being made strong, tough, and hard as a diamonds, when God completes this magnificent work of art in and on you, you will be ready to be presented, you will be ready to be in the show case, you will be shining so bright you will be glistening so the world can see you, because you are shining, you will draw people to you, so that special someone will also be attracted to you and he will pick you as his "Ruth" because he was God ordained for you, and only you. He is the only man that will compliment you.

THE L. 5P. K's MEN

These are the men who are the L. 5P K's. These are for the men that is truly ready to walk in what and where the Lord wants you. These are distinct offices. The L stands for Leaders or those who are striving to be leaders, the 5P's stands for Priest, Prophet, Providers, Protectors, Power and the K stands for Kings. These are the kind of men God wants to give as gifts to his daughters, these are strong men.

As a Leader, he will be able to take care of his home and business, he will be a good example for others to follow he will take care of any necessary responsibilities to lead his home and family, will be tough enough to lead and follow through on any responsibilities God gave him to rule over.

A Protector: will protect his family by all means necessary from danger, he is a praying man who is not a shame to go on his knees and inter seed

As a Provider, he will make sure his home and family come first and cared and provided for them always, he is a hard worker, God can entrust in his hands all he has given to him.

This man God gave you has Power, Power in the spirit to claim, just about anything he wants, he is not afraid to pray and intervene for his family, he will be that main intercessor in all areas, when you have this man at home you also will have power through the spirit as you come on one accord. The scripture says one may put a thousand to flight but with two ten thousand. You will be his help mate as the scripture says in Genesis, you are there to help cover him when he is weak, so he can stay focus and stable to continue seeking God for clear directions and guidance.

So, men continue to seek that diamond, and women continue to seek that gem so you both will shine and sparkle together bringing out the brilliance in each other.

Men you are the Priest over your home, one who goes to God on the behalf of his family and others, he makes sure things are in order and consults the Lord at all times. The Prophet of God, he uses you to have insight and gives specific instructions and answers to you for your family and others to do what is best for your house.

Finally, K is for the King, brothers remember God gave you women as a gift, you are gifts for each other, gifts to complement each other and to make each other happy she is that proverb 31 woman. Treat her like a queen do not take her for granted and she will in turn treat you like that king that you are. A king has dominion and authority. This is the order God wants that is best for your relationship and you, it is ordained, you are compatible with each other, and again you will be able to work through any storms come both your way.

One final word to my brothers, because you are the men of God, and you are the head and leaders, it is imperative to wait and choose the "right" woman in your corner, the right relationship. She is to be that supportive, one who will encourage and build you up ,she is a praying woman to cover you, not a nagger, she is that "help mate" .we know you are under pressure; we know the enemy is after you and is working overtime to destroy what you are called to be and to do.

CHAPTER 6
UNEQUALLY YOKE RELATIONSHIPS FOR SINGLES

Our unequally yoke relationships are on the rise, you are probably wondering what this means. I will attempt to give the simplest explanation so it will not be so confusing. In this case, it is when a Christian and a Non-Believer join together in union. Some of the many reasons are because our Christian singles will not wait on God for that person that is ordained for them.

Most of our sisters they are unable or impatient to wait because there are not many Christian men in the churches. Men outnumber women about three to one, most men in the churches are married, and if they are single Christians men most are looking elsewhere, and others most are in jails or prisons. Based on recent statistical data, for everyone hundred women in jail or prisons there are one thousand men behind bars, and for everyone hundred women died from suicide or homicide, there are five hundred plus men in the same category. or overcome by the pressures of life and committing suicide. Most of our Christian women complains of being tired of waiting years for a mate and become very impatient so they just settle, some settle because they like what they see, tall dark and handsome, or he has a nice body thinking they can change or convert these men once they are living with them or married to them.

Now most of our brothers that are singles prefer to choose women outside of the church, just settling because the woman looks good, she is "stack" she has a large chest, small waist and big buttocks, they live together also thinking they can change or convert these women, not realizing the consequences later, the relationship will last only so long because if you get into a relationship for the wrong reasons it will fail soon or later, if it is superficial and fleshly that will fail, body will get old and worn out of shape then what?. Most stay in relationships knowing that it is failing, because they put a lot of time, years and money with that one person, so now when it is time to move on they rather stay in that failing dead end relationship rather than to start over, they prefer to go through they arguing, fighting, disrespect and at times physical abuse, because it is easier to stay in the old relationship because they are used to that persons ways and personality, rather than starting over.

Both men and women cannot bear to be alone, instead they just settle, and they will not spend time with God to heal their broken hearts and hurts so that He will prepare and send the right person, instead they rather look on their own not knowing the true intents of the hearts and mind of a person, and they continue making the same mistakes repeatedly. Why would you give your heart to someone who will not respond to you in the same way?

Sisters and Brothers, do you not realize that your heavenly father loves you and wants the best for you? He said in 2 Corinthians 6 verses 14 "Be ye not unequally yoked together with unbelievers". But let me clarify this, not because you are a Christian and is in a union with another Believer does not always mean you are equally yoke in every area's in relationships. This does not only include "Personal Relationships" it also includes some of the following areas:

Your Personal Relationship, Your Personal Spiritual Walk, Your Personal Belief and Religion, Business Ventures, Levels of Education.

Relationships

In your relationships, this is your first area of concern is your relationships, if you are a Christian and you are involved in relationship either courting, dating or marriage with a non-believer your relationship is unbalanced and it will cause conflicts in your relationship and with your walk with the Lord, the scripture says "can two works together except they be agree" Amos 3 verses 3.

This is because of your lifestyle and your beliefs, if you are a follower of Christ and the person you are dating or married to is not a believer and has a different belief you will have many disagreements, and conflicts, and misunderstandings. Your thoughts will be different when it comes to spirituality, levels of integrity different, character may vary, your personal spiritual walk with the Lord, the maturity levels, because when it comes to issues to be resolved they will attempt to resolved them based

on a fleshly way of how they feel or their way of thinking instead of the biblical principles these views can be totally opposite from each other. This also includes people in your close personal circle of relationships such as friends.

Now if you are in a relationship with another Christian as you are, you can still be in an unequally yoke relationship, you may be asking the question or even wonder how is that possible if we are both Christians? Yes! this may be surprising, but it is true because of everyone personal spiritual walk with the Lord, one may be on a higher level and has a closer more serious relationship and the level of maturity because they spend more time with the Lord studying by reading his word and attending bible study and services getting more wisdom. They sacrifice time to volunteers in area's to find their purpose of where God what them to be.

During this time of a closer personal spiritual walk with the Lord, you are being changed into a new person it effects your way of thinking, the way you feel, and your passion becomes a total life changing experience, it will reveal your true purpose here on earth the reason for living and why you are here, the reasons he created you before he brought your parents together into existence. He made you specifically for a special work to be done only by you and no matter how small or insignificant it seems to you it is to glorify the Lord and to help someone else in this life or else you will never be happy or full filled in your life until you do something.

Religion

Religion is another big area of concern, when you are contemplating entering into a relationship with someone of a different religious beliefs and practices. Most people think because they are religious it is all the same, but I am here to let you know it is not the same. You must be very careful not because they are religious like you that does not make you equally yoke, again be careful the enemy sets all kinds of traps, do not fall for what you see with your eye it can deceive you, ladies do not fall for Mister "tall dark and handsome" because he is religious and do not have a relationship, men do not fall for the "coca cola bottle shape" the devil will send them too to throw you off course, and your focus diminished, remember "looks are deceiving, do not judge the book by its cover.

Business Ventures

If you are planning to venture out into business, you must pray first and ask the Lord for direction ask for guidance, ask if this person is the right person to venture out into business with and wait for an answer, get peace about it, again not because they are a Christian, or Non-Christian religious means it is the right person to do business with. Some goes into businesses with family not seeking God's direction first and later realize their mistakes, just because they are blood related does not mean they are the right match for you in business. Do not just jump in because it sounds good or it is a good offer, do not go in because they are friends , you must know if they have the same passion and drive as you to succeed , or they willing to work hard, are they lazy and are slacker and expect to get half of all that come in and they do not put the time in, you must find out about their business Ethics, character and if they have integrity.

Yes! a business relationship is just like a marriage, you will make decisions together, you will disagree to agree and will respect and confer with each other before you do anything concerning business decisions. It also depends on their level of maturity or experience. The scripture says "can two walks together except they be agree" Amos 3 verses 3.

Levels of Education

Yes! your levels of education can affect your relationships, let us be real, most of the time it is all about the amount of money you make and or are bringing home, when it comes to some relationship, it should not be so, but it is reality. It's about "Status" your career, and not about what is in a person heart, their potential and ambition in life to move forward, it's mostly about material things, their thinking and a person beliefs and relationship in serving and living for the Lord.

Be very cautious! Some people are happy with their careers and jobs and do not want to go back to school, to school to advance themselves, this can cause some conflicts too if they do not discuss it and agree.

CHAPTER 7
SINGLES WITH CHILDREN

In this section specifically I am speaking to non-believers and believers no one is exempt when it comes to protecting yourself from heart break and ending up in bad relationships.

For my single sisters and brothers with children seeking to enter back into the dating or courting arena again, I am extremely compassionate towards you, I know this must be hard for you and your children starting over and being very cautious of whom you bring or trust around your little angels. But continue to be very cautious and investigate who you decide to date, or get married to in the future, because there are many unscrupulous people, sexual predators out there prying on innocent children.

Seek a individual who is compatible with you who has children or one who may not have children but loves children and wants children in the future. Be wise use wisdom doing your best to check out background history before you get into a serious relationship and introduce or expose your children to them, your children should be more important to you than any man or woman you find yourself with in a relationship, be vigilant.

Divorced Singles

If you are one of the many divorced singles, who are seriously thinking about dating or courting again and you believed you are ready to commit into a relationship, make sure you wait for at least one to two years after your divorce this will give you time to heal, time to get your mind and heart clear if you were to reconcile and rekindle into your previous relationship, make sure are prayed up and are ready to get involved into another relationship, make sure you are waiting on the Lord to guide you into the right relationship with the right person, be especially sure you are ready emotionally, you do not want to enter into a relationship on a rebound, it is not fair to the other individual if you are not healed completely from the past chaos are you could take your frustrations out on them when situation arises that may cause stress or pressure. You do not want to get involved with someone who is on a rebound, that is not good for you are them, because they are emotionally unstable and is unable to make a clear decision, you would be setting up yourself to get hurt.

You do not want to get involved with someone just because you are lonely, hurt or in need. If you were in an abusive relationship weather it was physical, verbal, sexual this takes time to heal, if you fell you need counseling get help talk to someone about it so you can get well, go ahead it is alright, do let anyone talk you out of getting help or say you are crazy for getting help, do not think you are crazy for getting help, after all you were the one who went through the abuse they were not there.

Before you move forward into any relationship from a divorce make sure are working on all lose ends issues that need to be closed, such as financial, so you can leave the past behind and start anew.

Caution: Do not let family or friends push or talk you into any relationships or anyone else tries to rush you in especially if you are not ready, take your time, do not let your age be a factor, as the saying goes " the time clock is running out" because you have no children or just want companionship to release the loneliness pushes you into something you may regret later, regardless if you have never been married before or have been divorce each individual need to make an inventory of your life to see if you are just seeking a relationship to full fill the void or someone to make you happy, you are making the wrong decision, you are getting ready to break someone's heart that will eventually ends into a painful situation because you or that person was only there to fill avoid until they figure out what they want, also no one can full fill you and make you totally happy, you make each other happy because in any relationship there must be give and take.

So, in order to avoid all these problems, it is best to be patient until the Lord guides you to him or her. Do you realize the majority of the time when you feel lost or lonely and you seek after someone or something to fill that void, do you know it is because we Lord's presence in our lives, we need to fill that void and nothing you do will quench that desire until you acknowledge Him, therefore we end up hurting innocent people sometimes because we think it is people we need. Once you find that direction you will have peace.

Single Business Professionals

I cannot stress this enough, it is crucial that you ask and wait on God for guidance when it comes to relationships, we see only with our eyes, but God knows the hearts and minds of a person. I pray that he sends you someone like minded as you are, not someone who wants "status" only and someone who wants you for what you have, it is scary to think all you have worked hard for, and all the Lord have blessed you with, if you lined yourself up with the wrong person or make a wrong choice could cost you everything. This is why it is vital you do your homework and take your time.

Examine the heart, remember what comes out of the mouth comes from the heart. Brothers, I am not trying to hurt you or be hard on you, I know you have great taste for things that look good on the outside, seek that too, but look for one with a heart and a head on her shoulders, be real with yourself if you are looking for a real or long-term relationship, you must do some things too. You too must be very cautious as men and women in business, because you already know most are materialistic and they are looking for "things" security, people that are financially stable and are established. There are still good people out there, but you must be careful until He sends you that special person so you will both enjoy life together and be happy.

Singles Only for God's Purpose

To all my fellow sisters and brothers in Christ, I applaud you for your commitment to God and his work, I encourage you to continue you will be greatly rewarded, God bless you and I pray that His prosperity continues to flow in every area of your life. It is your choice not to have human companionship in order to serve the Lord whole heartedly free from commitment from others, so you would be totally committed and focused to the one and only love of your life, the Lord, just as the Apostle Paul, do not let anyone talk you out of serving God, if this is the way you choose to serve him stay focus and do not let anyone tells you different do not let anyone talk you out of serving Him this way, do not let them tell you are "crazy" for living this way and not wanting to have a family or other companionship, but if you are not able to abstaining from sexual sins.

The scripture says, "It is best to marry than to burn" Again I encourage you to continue doing that great work He calls you to do, continue to do the work of an evangelist, preacher, teacher and missionaries spreading the good news of the gospel saving and guiding the lost. I will continue to travail and intercession for your strength, boldness and perseverance. As you continue to walk after the things pertaining to Gods will for your life and destiny, continue in prayer and fasting, so when times of weakness or loneliness comes the enemy will not be able to tempt you to second guest yourself and God if you are doing the right thing or if it is worth doing what you are doing? or thus, what do I have to show for my hard work? Again, great will be your reward in this life.

CHAPTER 8
AGE DOES IT OR DOES NOT MATTERS

In relationships, the majority of the time we tend to think that the age of a person matters, but it depends on each individual and what they are looking for in a relationship and in a person.

Factors of most importance is the "heart", and it depends on the person's maturity of everyone's mind set. In fact, in reality it also depends on each individual life experiences and how they handle conflicts and trials and responsibilities of life.

Age is just a number, but it is maturity that really counts. It is not the numbers that we once believed in the past, People would normally say a person is mature because they are a certain age, while in fact as I get older, I realize when it comes to maturity level and age, some people that is up in age forties, fifties or sixties act and behave more in mature than individuals in their thirties and even twenties, again it depends on each individual mind set, maturity and unique experiences, regardless of their age, regardless if they are male or female, some people cannot seems to get themselves and lives together.

Do not get deceived and hung up on age, this does not mean just because a person is younger that they are in mature and have not got it together, or an older person is more mature because of their age, we would hope so, being the age that they are and the experiences they have been through, do not make an uneducated decision in a relationship based on some ones age. It also depends on every individual whether they like an older or a younger person that is up to you.

If you are searching for a long-term relationship, my advice to you would be to choose maturity over age, because in the long run when life situations come up, they will know how to handle them in

addition to their character that shows the real inner beauty of that person, that is key.

CHAPTER 9
SINGLES COUGH UP INTO THE DATING LIMBO

Singles, be wise, do not get caught up into the "dating limbo" especially if you are a child of God, what I mean by this is, if you find yourself in a ongoing relationship for more than two years heading nowhere, you have been courting or dating for several years and is unable or unsure if this is the right person for you or if this is truly the person you want to commit to and married for the rest of your life, no one wants to make a decision either to marry or break up and go their separate ways.

If they are unsure, they want to set a date for marriage, they are not sure if they love each other or just cough up into emotions. It should not take ten years to find out if this person is compatible with you are not, and if you believe the longer time, you spend you will know everything about that person, you will not. It should not take more than one to two years to know if the person you dating is or is not the one, over this time is just a waste of your time, it is time to break free.

In the time, you spend time together, you should already know and evaluated theirs and your likes and dislikes, if they just want to have a casual friendship, and just hung out together, or just want a sex partner with no commitment of marriage in the future, just companionship, because they do not want to be lone. I am not telling you to rush and not to find out all you can about a person before you jump into marriage and make one of the biggest mistakes of your life, but there must be a limit, and a point in time when you should know. after several years of being into this kind of relationship, you will find yourself falling into temptation and sexual gratification, we all know the flesh is weak, and God is not pleased with this, that is why it is best to move on and find someone who wants a true long-term relationship leading into marriage.

If you are not familiar with the old cliché that says" why buy the cow if you can have the milk for free" It simply means if you are already living together like husband and wife, why would they want to commit to a real marriage, you make it easy so they will not settle and commit to you. Most of the time in these relationships they usually end up leaving and marring someone else. Someone must be the brave person to make the decision, because you are in a dead-end relationship going nowhere, and while you are wasting time, losing years and getting old with someone you know is not the one, God may have already prepared and have the right person for you, but because you are involved in this "Limbo" they either passed you by or the Lord will not allow them to come your way. So, ask God for strength and boldness to do what you must do to move forward, move on do not let God's blessing pass you by. Many times, we as individuals blame God for not answering our prayers, but in fact it is on us we do not seems to realize that it is not Gods fault majority of the time for unanswered prayers, He is waiting on us to move out of the way so He can send the blessings, but we are too blind, stubborn and disobedient to see that we are the one's standing in the way hindering our own blessings. If you are men or women let them, go stop blocking your true blessings, they are hindrance to you especially when you are doing kingdom work, if you do not let them go, He will eventually move them for you.

Cough Up in Emotions

Emotions will sometimes lead to sexual indiscretions, followed by money, and material gain, no one wants to start of their relationship this way, these relationships usually do not last, because the relationship is based off of things and not love. Sexual gratification is only temporary once this is played out, after a while there is nothing left to fall back on to continue the relationship, then it falls apart leaving unhappiness, misery, confusion, and a broken heart.

CHAPTER 10
CELEBRATING SPECIAL OCCASIONS DURING COURTSHIP

Celebrating special occasions during courtship and dating is very important, because as the relationship leads into marriage these kinds of behaviors should follow into the relationship also, it should not be one sided when celebrating or in general nothing in your relationship should be one sided. you may be wondering what I mean, it simply means if you are celebrating Christmas, valentine's day, other than two or three other occasions that only one person celebrates or a birthday unless you both have the same birthday. It should not be the men only giving a gift or spending money, it is two people in the relationship it should be shared unless stated and there is an agreement between the two.

If the relationship become one sided in not just special occasions it will also become one sided in other things and the relationship will start to get boring, if you are the one always giving, eventually you will feel as if you are being used and are taken for granted, when you are entering a relationship there should not be any more Me, Myself and I. Because after a while resentment starts to set in. Remember if you want a long-lasting relationship, you cannot be selfish and it's all about me. I cannot stress this enough, Ladies be wise, treasure him, if you treat him like a king, he will in return treats you like his queen, as you continue to court and date once you transition into marriage the way you treat each other during this stage should follow and continue.

CHAPTER 11
TAKE TIME TO TALK

Simply taking time out of your busy schedule to talk with each other, or take time to write down your thoughts on paper and give it to your courting partner so they can read it on their own time, when you write things down, you can express yourself better, you can convey things in writing such as your likes and dislikes, in general things that bothers you the most. Some time we take for granted words expressed on paper, reveals a lot more than in person, because you forget things and when you write them down it reveals the true feelings, believe writing your thoughts down on paper take time and special attention, writing things down make a statement that this is more urgency of more importance to take a look further, because communication is key and is vital in any relationship it is important to practice and learn these skills before you transition further, it is necessary it is a must, it can make or break your relationship, do not wait until your partner is frustrated, upset and tired then you want to talk this is the worst time to talk and you should not wait until it build up to this point to talk, it may be too late they have their minds made up and do not want to be bothered.

Listening

As it is with communication, listening goes hand in hand, you need to listen to each other not just hear each other. A person knows when you are listening and being attentive, good eye to eye contact and your verbal responses, and your body language. One person cannot do all the talking and no listening or the opposite, when you hear each other, it usually goes out one ear and out the next, this is called ignoring, this is hurtful and disrespectful as if you were not there, you do not want this in your relationship.

Anger

You cannot pretend that you will never get angry at each other because you are courting, no matter how you try you will go through periods of anger, this is part of life, you will not always have it easy, part of this is either misunderstanding or miscommunication or ignoring a person.

The scripture says not to let the sun go down before you resolve this issue, again it leads back to communication. If you must walk away, and calm down to prevent argument go, it gives you time to clear your head and rethink things over, it will also change the tone, sometimes it not what you say, it is how you say it.

Do not make rash decisions in anger, walking helps to release tension and stress you will have a more rational that helps you see things differently, sometimes during these walks, you will see things differently during your time of thinking things over, sometimes you realize you are the one who blew things out of proportion, you were a bit touchy and took things the wrong way, or just a bad day, be honest with yourself, ask the Lord to help you with these short comings and to forgive you, then forgive yourself, then come back and break that pride and ask for forgiveness, and talk, this is a good habit to practice and carry over into marriage. Always get God involved to help direct you how to approach and to resolved issues, if one partner is still angry leave it alone until both has calm down and then talk.

CHAPTER 12
DO NOT CRY IT IS FOR YOUR GOOD

Sometimes in our lives we get coughed up and jump into relationships that were not the best for us, and by the time you realize the mistake is already done and you cannot undo it. We all make mistakes in our lives, but hopefully it is not detrimental, hopefully we learn from our mistakes. Even with the best intentions in a relationship seeking the opposite sex, we think we are doing good and next thing you know they are unfaithful to you, and you get kicked to the curb and you do not know why, you being transparent as you are did not see what you have done wrong to deserve this, and you did not see it coming, you cannot figure out why things happen the way they did, but because we are so blinded, It is because of our own immaturity and level of spiritual walk, God see's all things, He sees what we cannot see, do not cry! Do not get bitter, instead get better, prepare yourself instead of getting impatient and looking, stop! because while you are looking in the wrong direction,

God has sent them to look for you, but because your eyes is gazing else where you are unable to see them looking at you.

Some Christians have their eyes in the world, looking at flesh only, outer beauty alone instead of the entire package, a heart after God first, second mind set, third outer appearance, uses them to push you out, so He can push you over, He uses them to push you out so He can push you in; this means that He pushes you where you needs to be so you can win the victory in the relationship battle, because He sees it would cause more harm than good so He turns it around for your good, because God uses that bad experience to make you more mature, alert, aware and sensitive and also to help others in the future. So, He pushes you into the right relationship with the right person that means you well, when some of these relationship ends we cannot see clearly, you only feel hurt and heart aches while your blessing was in disguise He saves you from all these, this is nothing compares to what was waiting ahead, and because He sees ahead of you and interrupt the plans of the enemy to cause you more pain or even destroys you, but God seeks to save you, because you are precious in his sight. This could have pushed you over the edge causing you to give up on people, and on any close personal relationships again, causing you to lose your faith, confidence, hope and trust in anyone because of your past bad relationships. Do not give up, God has someone for everybody, it is probably not your time or season yet, for Mr. or Mrs. right.

You must be asking how much longer must I wait? you must remember God do not work on a schedule or our time clock, and he is working on you to "heal" you from some of the past hurts, he need to get rid of some things he sees in you that need changing and cleaning, He wants you to have some space and time for yourself to sort things out and put them in order, before you proceed into the next relationship. He is also working on, changing, and cleaning some things on the mate to come. I want you to take a moment and imagine where you are presently in your life, your mind set, emotionally, spiritually, be real and honest with yourself, if you were to get involved right now jumping into a relationship would it last? could you treat that person honestly, as you would like them to treat you? could you honestly do everything a committed relationship requires? if all these answers is yes, and you were honest, then I believe you are ready. If not you will mess up that person, and drive them away. So, wait a bit and get yourself ready so you both will complement each other in the appropriate time.

CHAPTER 13
PICNIC AT THE PARK

Whenever you are in a relationship, especially one that is becoming serious and you both are discussing commitment, make sure there is no other person involved and you are number one, make sure he or she is the only one, again do not be in a rush as per desperation, loneliness or just fair of being a lone make sure you don't compromise and just settle, and you become the "spare tire" make sure during your dating or courtship, if you find out the individual you are dating is seeing someone else other than you, you need to take responsible actions and make sure you become number one, make sure he or she make a decision on your behalf and if they do not, you make that decision, and walk away from that relationship, do not let anyone use you and play with your emotions, again guard your heart., because if you continued in a relationship like that it is unhealthy and will lead to bitterness and resentment to the opposite sex in future relationships, It will also lower your self-esteem, it will also blurred your judgment for future relationships causing you to miss out on the "right person" when they come along you will not be able to judge if it is real or a facade, the longer you stay into it, the more pain it will cause, because of the ties, and the harder it gets to break apart. Never deliberately put yourself into situations such as this thinking you have control, and you can change or win them over. Again, you are only setting up yourself to be hurt and to be the "spare tire". Do not settle for less you are precious, we are not perfect we get weak sometimes and fall in traps, but if you know ahead of time do not walk into it, walk away from it.

CHAPTER 14
THE TRANSITIONAL PHASE

Now that you are in the transition phase into a deeper and more committed to the relationship eventually leading into marriage. At this stage you both should have already be transparent to yourself and to each other, you should already know what you are looking for in the relationship and in the person, you are now proposed or engaged by now you both should know a majority of the likes and dislikes. Just a reminder, one of the biggest misconception most couples have is a false expectation of when they get married the person will make them completely happy and everything will be "peaches and cream" they tend to forget that Jesus must be the center of their lives to bring true happiness, and they must make themselves happy, and in turn make each other happy.

As a soon to be married couple you both must seek counseling, and should already being counseled, some people may ask why, it is not because you are having problems during your courtship, it is for further exploration into questions they may ask both of you that is very important you both never thought of to ask each other, and also there might be things that you hold dare in believing a man or a woman should be responsible for, that you both may have disagreements on that may cause you to rethink or may stop the relationship from going any further, in general in counseling they want to make sure you know what you are getting yourself into, it is long term and should be for a lifetime weather it is good or bad, and not just "here today gone tomorrow". You both do not want to be a part of the statistics; the divorce rate is presently at 70% and the failure rate for all first-time marriages is at 51% I cannot stress enough each individual must be honest with themselves and with the individual they are planning to marry, there should not be any hiding of anything, you should be up front, be open, be yourself and put it all on the table. If you notice that you are unable to be yourself around the person you are courting this may be a sign this is not the right person for you. It does not make sense to start a relationship with lies, eventually it will surface, and you will be caught.

Ask Hard Questions Before You Transition into Marriage

There should be openness to talk about past, present and future! past relationships, money, freedom to be open and communicate, jobs and career paths, your desires and goals for the future, dealing with past debts before marriage, splitting bills and expenses when you are married, having credit cards, budget savings percentages for each individual each pay period, opening checking and savings accounts together or separate, changing careers and returning to school to further education and only one income is coming in, and there is only one person working while one stays home for family purposes, or an agreement made between both of you, one income is enough to support both people comfortably, or he or she wants you to sign a prenuptial agreement, will there be a problem if the woman makes more money.

This is where hard questions should come in, think of questions to ask and write them down, give them open-ended ones, make up scenarios and see what the responses would be, examine the responses and answers carefully. For example, if I lost my job, and it is only one income coming in, and all the financial responsibilities shift to you and the money coming in is just enough to make ends meet and it is slow finding work, how would you handle the situation? Will they help and support you if you have plans for the future to have your own business, would you like to have children in the future, if so, how many, future plans to buy a home together.

Other questions that need to be discussed are some past and present checkups, such as some of these, most people overlook because they are so in love.

Habits, addiction or background check ups, they forget to tell you about. Some of these are, drugs, alcohol, pornography, Pedi files (child molester) bisexuality, smoking, gangs, gambling.

You both need to get tested for any sexually transmitted diseases before you get married to protect yourselves, they may or may not know they have contracted something in their past relationships.

Finally, once again, most of their character should already be revealed, but if not keep a close eye on them, look for these traits and see if they are men and women of their words and by their actions, see if he is "mamma's boy" or "daddy's girl" see if they lies a lot, stingy, selfish, lazy, untidy, jealous, motivated, sneaky, steals, holds grudges, prejudice, vindictive, revengeful, a hard worker and have a mind set to be their own boss in the future.

As you transition into marriage, you must continue to do the same things to keep each other's attention as you did during your courtship to keep your marriage fresh and add spice to the relationship, this is one reason some marriages fail, because they loss the spice and stop doing for each other as they did in the beginning during courtship.

CHAPTER 15
PRESERVATION FOR COUPLES THE MARRIAGE RELATIONSHIP

Now that you have entered marriage, it is beautiful, you are newlyweds, and everyone is happy and in love. You should also remember this, any union God puts together the enemy will always try to drive a wedge between and tries to separate them, but it is up to both of you to communicate and get rid of any misunderstandings immediately, put away pride and childish behaviors, and work through things no matter what it is to keep your love and marriage together.

It is important to continue to be courteous and kind to each other, In the morning when you both wake up greet each other with hugs and kisses before you leave home, and if you have not already established making phone calls at least once per day just to say, I was thinking about you or I want to let you know I love you, and you mean a lot to me, you want to let them know you appreciate them, it does not matter how long you are married, e-mails or text messages is good but a phone call is the best because it is more personal and intimate, the other messages cannot replace hearing a voice.

When they come home in the evening hug and greet them with a kiss again, edify each other, so you both feel special. A date night, game night, and movie nights, during the week should also be established, if not do so as soon as possible it helps to keep the spice into the relationship, continue by giving each other cards, flowers, gifts during birthdays, anniversaries and during nonspecial occasions too.

Share the chores at home together, be considerate of each other, remember you both work, if one reach home before the other start dinner or if you cannot cook bring something home or take turns one week at a time, one week you cook and the next he or she cooks, take time for each other by running his or her bath water once in a while take turns it is not a one-way relationship give a foot bath to each other once in a while it is the personal touch that means a lot.

Compromise with each other if there is something you both cannot agree on. As the years increase in your relationship you should be falling in love with each other, not falling apart and falling out of love with each other.

Make your marriage romantic, you can role play with each other if you are into this or just simply find your own ways to keep the spice in your relationship to keep the flames lit. There are some women, that still wear rollers in their hair at nights, there is nothing wrong with wearing rollers, but if you are home during the days or if you are taking care of the children a stay home mom or grandmother, take those rollers out and style your hair. Do not walk around the house all day in your house coats, dusters or your nightgowns, do not let your husband come home and see you the same way he left you in the morning.

Get rid of those old torn up night gown and under wears and those old fashion grandmother's sleep wears and under wears, buy something different, wear something sexy to surprise him once in a while do not let him get" board "and tired of seeing you into the same outfit too often. Ladies, I know as we get older our bodies changes, but I cautioned you, do not continue to deny or push your husbands away sexually unless you are going through medical problems and he knows about them, and you are under physician care or you are on your monthly cycle, stop giving him excuses and complaining, this goes for men too that are holding out on their wives. Stop it! Do not hold out on each other, if you continue eventually, you will cause the enemy to come in and destroy your relationships.

If you are Christians nothing should change, not because you are, does not mean the romance should change or cease, it should be just as spicy as you both desire to keep each other happy. The scripture said, "marriage is honorable in all and the bed undefiled" Hebrews 13 verses 4. This basically means, a married couple should do whatever you both desires, and what you as couple does behind closed doors that make you happy and give you pleasure, God gives you the okay. Spend quality time together relaxing, and listening to clean, soft romantic music that is meaningful, and fun filled for both of you.

Spending Meaningful Time Together On Outings

As newlywed couples, even if you are not newlyweds, it is a good idea to take vacations at least once or twice per year spending some meaningful quality time together. I know we are in a "recession "and time is hard, people are losing their jobs there's not a lot of money coming in, just for this purpose with all the stress around you this should make it even more beneficial, to get away relax, and recoup. Start a small budget plan, put away a certain amount from each person's pay checks each week for one year, figure out where you want to go, and what you want to spend and budget from this, set aside a special savings account specifically for this purpose only, or you can use your income taxes each year. There are many other things or trips you both could take together that will not break the bank or cost a significant amount of money.

Many times, we do not think about these things because we are too busy or stressed out worrying about everything else. This is one way of keeping spice and fire in the relationship, making you feel as though you are dating or courting again. As couples these are some of the things you can do.

Weekend Excursions

Go on a weekend excursion, it is not too expensive a plan was you both want to visit locally, out of the city or out of state, then reserve a room or suit for the weekend and drive to your destination, driving gives a sense of relaxation, and sightseeing. When you get to your destination, tour the city on your own or use tour guides, the local newspapers are good guides to show what's going on locally around town, go visit museums, art exhibits, and other things the city may offer.

Day Trips

Go on day trips, do some sightseeing in your local city, do and see things you are normally too busy to do on a regular basis. Take a cruise to nowhere if you both are home for the day. Take long walks on the beach or on the lake holding hands, and watch the sun set. Rent or go watch movies for the day. Go and get a relaxing couples massage or a manicure and pedicure. Go and take a trip to the amusement park for the day, date night at least once per week before the weekends.

Picnics

Most people forget about the good old days, most young couples thinks this is boring and cheap, but if you are saving and is on a budget this will enable you to spend some quality time together, find a different park you have never been before, it brings a sense of romance because the different atmosphere, then prepare a picnic basket with a cooler find a big shade tree spread out your blanket and relax and talk, parks are not only for riding bikes or taking the kids to play.

Fishing

If you are the kind of couple who like the outdoors, going fishing on a lake, beach or river is a great outdoor activity, you can spend time together, it's fun and it cost hardly anything.

Bowling

Bowling is another fun activity you both could enjoy together and have a great time, it gives you the opportunity to spend quality time together having fun, and it does not cost a lot when you are on a budget.

Game Rooms

If you both love to play games, there are games rooms in almost every city, it's fun and again gives couples time to spend together, it is very inexpensive, some game rooms consist of a variety of games and activities such as pool.

Movies

Plan a romantic evening out, make reservations at one of your favorite restaurants or one you always wanted to visit and after the movie go for a late evening dinner. you should make time to go out to dinner or the movies, try go to see a drive-in movie if you never been before, it is old fashion but could be very romantic too, do these at least once a month. There are some Restaurants that have live entertainment, such as music, you could both have a great time together having dinner and dancing.

Concerts and Plays

Occasionally surprise him or her to a play or to a concert to see their favorite artist perform again if money is tight, it will take special planning ahead of time budgeting for special occasions as these, but it will be well worth it, these are quality time spend together that money cannot buy, and memories that will last for a long time.

Games

On occasions, surprise him or her to their favorite pass time. Whether it is basketball, football, baseball, tennis or soccer, again if the funds are tight plan a head and budget, this is quality time you will both enjoy spending together and the memories will last a lifetime.

Long Afternoon Drive

Sometimes taking long drives is very relaxing, especially on a Sundays afternoon after church service, it is soothing, just drive it does not need to be planned, do not just run home to the same boring routine, stop and have dinner in a town you never been in before and after wards stop by an ice cream pallor and have dessert.

CHAPTER 16
SETTING THE MOOD AND THE ATMOSPHERE

Keeping the spice and romance in your relationship should not be too hard, simply because you both should already know their likes and dislikes, you should basically know what they want and how to please him or her and each other, even if you are both newlyweds, it just takes time and practice.

Setting the mood basically depends on you and how you start your day, it could be a provocative kiss you gave each other in the morning before leaving for work and having them reminisce throughout the day. Or before you leave for work in the morning you kiss them goodbye into your birthday suite or the launderers' underwear you put on in the morning before you left for work, or the quick teaser you gave each other that morning before you left for work or the sweet tease provocative phone calls you made to him or her during the day when you call to say hello, or just wait until they come home and surprise them at the door.

As a couple, both men and women need to do these things for each other to set the atmosphere and mood with mellow or soft romantic music. Prepare his or her bath water, have soft or low lighting, or you can use fragrant scented candles this stimulate the senses, and if it is a special occasion set the bedroom with rose pedals and candles.

Also, you can have their favorite meals as the clichés go's "The way to a man's heart is through his stomach" this simply means that a man loves a woman who knows how to cook his dinner and feed him, especially a well-balanced homemade meal from the woman he loves, you will defiantly capture his heart, if you cook his or her favorite dish, occasionally, set the table with fresh flowers and candles, make it special, at the time he or she is close to home you can surprise them at the door, or after they eat and take a bath you can slip on something new and sexy, something eye catching such as a negligee and a touch of his favorite perfume and a hint of her favorite cologne. Men, you need to know this about your woman, sometimes a woman just want to be cuddled, a gently touched, rub or massage and talk, it is very important to listen to her, it does not mean she do not want to make love, she just want to feel pampered and relax, then after a while she will respond to you, just because you are in the mood and you touch her, this does not mean she will automatically get turned on and is in the mood to make love, sometimes she is ready just be patient and give her time, it is do not rush, sometimes it is slow and gentle, and sometimes it is ruff it depends on what you both want or like.

If you are always in a rush and do not listen to her, she will feel as though you just need her only for sex. men, we know you are always ready when it comes to sex, but keep in mind, always try and keep her needs met too whatever they may be. Ladies, I cannot emphasize this enough to you, I know most men wants to make love 24/7 if possible.

It is your responsibility as a wife to keep him satisfied and his needs met as much as possible, you know him better than anyone, communicate with him, do not leave him longing, do not let him stray, again it is your responsibility as a wife to keep him happy sexually.

Too often, I hear some women making excuses, and "holding out" on their husbands they just do not feel like having sex, they are too tired, they have headaches, sorry to burst your bubble ladies, if you are tired take a nap get some rest and get up and satisfy your man, if you have a

headache take something for that headache, if you do not feel like it, top telling him not today and one day become two and two become a month and a month become a year, make it today, he is your husband, you married him you know his needs and desires full fill them and stop making excuses. Do not leave that door open and the enemy creeps in and destroys your marriage. So, continue to keep the fire burning in your relationships.

Married But Feels Single

This may occur for several reasons. The first is possibly because of the "spiritual significance" this might be missing in your life, this means that each individual is born to know God, and that spiritual connection is missing, and something inside of you is yearning and crying out to find that part that is missing, and nothing that you do, or find to do does not completely satisfy or nothing or no one can full fill that void, it is a sense of loneliness and longing that you just cannot seem to pinpoint directly. Only the Lord can full fill that empty feeling.

The second possibly is because of your husband or wife, if you are unequally yoke, one may be a believer and one may not or one may be more advanced than the other and there is a drifting away. The husband may not be doing his part, and the wife feels as though she is pulling the majority of the responsibilities, or it may be the opposite. With this try to find that balance and work through it together, and you need to find your "spiritual significance" no matter who agrees or disagrees with you, once you find it you will find peace.

Interracial or Mixed Marriages

Couples, I encourage and applaud you, Because of the society and the world we are living in today there are so many prejudices ', hate and violence, and pressures. If God brought you both together, do not let family, friends, society and some church people separate you if you are

Christians.

Remind yourselves of the vows you made to each other when pressures and hand hard times come. scripture says, who God has joined together let no man put asunder. we must be transparent and not superficial, and stop being hypocritical, as Christians and we wonder why the some of the unsaved do not want to come into our churches, this is because there is still some deep-rooted hate, prejudges and anger towards others that are not of the same cultures, race, or nationality instead of loving people for who they are. Couples continue loving the Lord and each other.

Family

Do not let family get involved in your relationships during times of disagreements, they will take sides and tear your relationships apart, do not let them give you advice as to how and what to do to handle situations, if it come to that point seek counseling elsewhere, some family means well but others does not, work thing out together by communicating with each other, give each other some personal space and time to themselves to think, both are unable to come to an agreement

or compromise again nothing is wrong with seeking professional advice, they will not take sides or discriminate.

Friends and Society

Friends should be the same as family when it comes to your relationships, you can tell them some things, but not everything you both need to conclude in resolving issues by communicating. Again, some friends mean well, and others do not, do not let them give you wrong advice, and do not let anyone cohere you into any decisions.

Children and A Place to Call Home

I know sometimes it is hard to ignore, do not be bothered by what people in society want to say, think or do, you cannot live your lives for people, live your lives to your fullest potential and be happy. If you decide to have a family, discuss and agree how many children you both want and be happy and love them.

Discuss and deciding where to buy a home, find a place you both will be happy, a place you call home, this is a big decision make sure you investigate the neighborhood the community be wise use wisdom and choose a good place where you both will be happy and safe.

Medical Issues in Marriages

As you both remember when you took your wedding vows, it states "for better or for worse". Many people especially some of the younger generations, feels that they are invincible when it comes to sickness or diseases, it does not matter if you are young, old or middle aged, sickness and diseases can strike anyone at any time, and we have no control over these events when they come. If you are a younger or an older couple in your marriage and one or both spouses have some form of illness or disease during your marriage, please be patient, support and work with each other until things get better, pray for each other daily no matter what is going on in your present situation. The scripture says that God is able to do abundantly above all that we ask or think.

Do not be selfish, take care of each other and God will take care of you, do not abandoned your spouse because of sickness, you would not want God to abandoned you in your times of needs.

In times like this, you need all the help you can get, especially prayers, He answer prayers no matter how bad it gets, no matter how far or near, do not be a shame to ask for prayers, scripture says "one may put a thousand to flight and two ten thousand".

Special Medical Issues

Sometimes we have issues diseases we have no control over, diseases we did not bring on ourselves, these are illnesses or diseases we inherited that has been passed down from generation to generation, especially some within the Afro American race, some of the are history of Hypertension (high blood pressure), Diabetes (high blood glucose), Menopause(changes), Erectile Dysfunction, Hysterectomy, Breast Removal, these issues effect both male and female.

Special Notes For Men Only

If you are a man and you are in this category as several thousand of these other men are, this is for you, do not be a shame, God saw and knows your pain, do not just sit and suffer alone in your private pain, I want to let you know there is hope, there is help available for you, I know it gets frustrating, if you are suffering from a medical issue such as hypertension, and you are taking medications that is causing or effecting you sexually from performing, low or no erection and you are unable to please or satisfy your spouses and you are both tired and frustrated, there is help! Most men are still a shame and put pride a head of their conditions they will not go and seek medical help.

Do you not know God made Doctors and other Specialist to help you, now a day with the advanced technology they can do so much more than in the past? So do not be afraid or a shame you did not cause these things on yourself, so do not let the enemy make you feel guilty , do not stay home and cry over it, do not keep it a secret, after all how can you keep it a secret, your wife already knows there is something wrong, go and get professional medical advice, it's not fear to your spouse if you do not at least try and get help, again, do not let these issues, because you are in denial, pride, shame and ignorance cause your relationship (marriage) to fall apart, I urge you to get help as soon as possible.

Special Notes Only For Women

My fellow sisters, I know we do not stay young forever, as we get older our bodies change, and we have our own issues to worry about. If you are at that age where your body is changing, and you are going through the "changes", This is the normal changes of life for us women, you need not to be a shame or afraid. Do not be in denial or prideful about this, if you are suffering severely you too need to seek professional medical help, through the years, they have found many natural and synthetic sources of medicine to help relive these "Hot Flashes" and vaginal dryness we women complain about, do not stay home and suffer in your own private pain, as I stated before, it's not private, because your husband already knows.

Do not let him suffer from sexual starvation because you are suffering, do not keep denying him and push him away. Do not let the lowered sexual desires or the vaginal dryness, cause discourse in your marriage get help. Another troublesome issue is Hysterectomy, and Mastectomy, or a complete removal of one or both breast, this is a hard thing for women, a feeling of less self-worth, lowered self-esteem, feeling less attractive, loss of femininity, and beauty as a female, self-conscious.

Ladies, be strong, I want to let you know, you are still beautiful in Gods eyes, and the greatest thing is this, no matter what is missing you still have life. And if God blessed you with a God fearing husband regardless of how you feel or how you look, he will still love you from the inside out, he will love you for you, regardless of what happens, just do not push him away because of how you feel he is already hurting because you are hurting and there is nothing he can do but pray for you and love you as you are.

CHAPTER 17
SPENDING QUALITY TIME WITH GOD

Every married couple needs to spend some quality time together with the Lord, either you do it now, freely or you will have no choice later when hard times come, you can do it together or as an individual.

Many times, we may say to ourselves, "I do not have time, or I do not know what to pray. It is for this very reason, I would like to share this with you, this may be of some help to you and your walk with the Lord.

Sacrifice

Sacrifice each morning, and set aside some quality time for the Lord, before starting your day, wake up at least fifteen minutes earlier, make this a habit and it will become part of you, pray and then read your word at least one chapter per day. As you go on your way ask God to reveal things to you and give you understanding of what you have read, and as you go through your day continue to meditate on the word this will make a difference in your lives, and you will see a change in your relationship with the Lord.

Daily Prayer Before Starting Your Day

Many times, we just do not know how and what to pray. Here is a prayer, you can use all or parts to fit where and what you want to cover when you pray. Father God, I come to you in the name of your only son Jesus, giving you all honor, glory and praise, forgive me of all my sins I committed known and unknown, as I also for give those who sin against me. I come humbly before you and let your perfect will be done in my life, order my footsteps through the day and teach me how and what to pray, teach me what to say, and what not to say, guide my actions. show me who to pray for, what to pray for, when to pray and where to pray! Lord, I cover myself with the blood of Jesus, and claim the protection for my extended family, husband, wife, children, purpose and destiny, gifts, ministry, church, pastors, finances, home, marriage, health, business, I surrender my mind, body, emotions, and spirit completely to you in every area of my life. I come against every work of the enemy in the name of Jesus, that would try to hinder me and my family from serving you, I canceled every assignment of attacks the enemy send and used by people, what they say or do, things, circumstances or situation. I give myself over to the true and living God who has all power and control, furthermore, I command Satan, and all principalities, powers, and rulers of darkness in the name of Jesus to leave my presence and anything pertaining to me, I break and tear down every strong holds, cover my families and children I claim every protection, as they go on the highways, in school on their jobs and these at home, I claim, peace, joy and prosperity, I will not be discouraged, or hold any anger, hate, envy, or bitterness towards anyone but will love them with the love of God in my heart, through the holy spirit. I surrender my life and all my earthly possessions to you, cleanse me from all unrighteous works that will prevent our close fellowship, give me persevering strength, knowledge, wisdom and understanding, thank you for answering my prayer in the name above all names Jesus   *Amen.*

CHAPTER 18
THE REALITY IN MARRIAGES

In order for couples to have a long-lasting relationship in their marriages, you both need to be serious about it, it is a must that you engage yourselves in spending quality time together getting to know each other more. It will take a lot of communication, talk things out and agree to disagree, remember you know each other better than everyone else. Caution. Do not take everyone's advice.

Be committed to prayers for your relationship (marriage) your spouse, yourself and to each other. Compromise, be humble and trust each other.

Humility

What is Humility? It is a state of being humble, absent of pride or self-assertion. For a long-lasting relationship in your marriage, humility is one of the keys to propel the relationship in many aspects of your marriage, you will have disagreements and at times one or both of you must walk away and calm down to prevent arguments or at times stay silent and do not utter a word, even when you know you are right, you cannot always have the last word! it is hard, but to keep the peace in your home and marriage, it is best to submit sometimes. If you are right, and you walk away and be submissive God will usually deal with your spouse's conscience when they are wrong, and if they are not too prideful, they will usually come and apologies.

Committed

To be committed means to bind as by a promise, a pledge, to engage or to make known the opinions or views of oneself on a issue. To make a committed is another very crucial link and keys to a lasting marriage, you must be committed to the relationship and to each other no matter what comes up against you and your spouse, in the good and bad times, and in times of struggles and trials. Never get up and leave your spouse during hard times. this is the time you need each other the most, it will also prove how strong you are and how strong your love is for each other. You should always keep in mind hard times do not last forever; I know while you are going through it seems as if it will never come to an end. but it does, with prayers, encouragement, support, and patience it will come to an end eventually. Scripture reminds us that God does not give us more than we can bear, my Lord, sometimes it does feel as if we just cannot with stand anymore! but the Lord knows all things.

Do you remember Job! what he went through, so if you are going through just continue to look up, God will see you through! and when it is all over, when you look back it will be just a memory. The Lord knows that you will make it. He reminds us again that "weeping may

endure for a night but joy comes in the morning".

Communications, Communication, Communication

What is communication? is the giving or exchanging of information or message as by talking, or writing. This is one of the most Important aspects of your relationship, this could make or break it, especially in times of trials we all need to take time out of our busy schedule to talk especially when it comes to pressing issues that need to be addressed or resolved immediately, do not wait and push these issues under the rug, it will only surface and escalate at a later time, causing frustration, anger and unnecessary stress while it could have been resolved by talking.

Men I know some of you have an issue with communication, but I urge you to take time and talk with your wives and not your friends or your family as if they are the one you have married, if it is important to you, you will find the time to talk. Most couples wait until the situation is blown out of proportion where there is no resolve left and counseling will not work at this point. I am encouraging you if problems arise resolve them as soon as possible between yourselves.

You cannot take anyone's advice especially if they are not of the faith or biblical. If it is at the point where outside help is needed, then you both need to seek professional Christian counseling that will build a gap between the two they will not be judgmental or will not take sides there will be a balance. You would not want to be a part of the growing statistics of failed marriages, it is now 51% of all first-time marriages fail, and we are now at a 70% divorce rate. just want to encourage you to work together and put your best into it.

Financial Problems

Financial problems are the number one killer of failed marriages or relationships, but again it comes down to lack of communication, make sure you both have a plan how to budget, what to budget and what to save and splitting bills. Again, it all comes down to communication and listening to each other, The bible says to be quick to hear and slow to speak, listening includes good eye to eye contact, no interruptions while the other person is speaking and asking questions after the person is finish speaking, good communication is also how you say things by your tone of voice and your body language or facial expression.

Trust

Trust is another very important key aspect of any relationship, especially in marriage. Trust is a firm belief or confidence in the honesty, integrity and reliability of another person or thing. Or faith and reliance on the person or thing trusted. If there is no trust in each other there will be no relationship or marriage. It will not last. As the cliché goes "action speaks louder than words". You should be able to trust someone not only by their words but by what they do, their actions.

Security

Security; Is the state of being or feeling secure; freedom from fear, anxiety, danger or doubt; a state or sense of safety or certainty. Security in a relationship is a woman number one priority, she loves to feel a sense of stability, and she like to feel that everything is going to be okay.

Love and Understanding

Learn and be understand to each other, and continue to love each other For a spouse that causes his or her marriage to fail because of total betrayal, loss of commitment, deceived by the enemy and went outside the boundaries of their relationship at home, he or she who committed this act beyond the boundaries of their marriage, they themselves must forgive themselves in order to go on and those spouses that was betrayed innocently, hurting and in pain, surprised and unable to understand what went wrong.

If you are reading this and has been in some similar situations or is in a situation that brings back painful memories, my empathy goes out to you, I understand this too shall pass, remember "weeping may endure for a night, but joy comes in the morning psalms" psalms 30 verses 5. Remember your morning is on its way, but to get through this the healing process must first take place through prayers and direction from the Lord. Forgiving yourself and the other person involved, if communication and counseling is not enough to resolve the issues in the marriage, then separation is inevitable, this is for total healing and it helps to give each other space and time to think things over, it is to prevent verbal and possibly physical abuse to each other due to the hurt and pain. Remember if there is no forgiveness there is no healing, and if there is no healing you will not be free to move on, holding unforgiveness will only give the person or persons ammunition to hold you hostage by the enemy, you give him or her power to hold you captive for a long time.

If you decide to get a divorce you will never be free from the baggage's of unforgiveness to love and trust again in the future. In addition, unforgiveness causes health problems, such as stress and anxiety that causes many medical issues and ailments in your body. Sometimes physicians are unable to diagnose or detect the root cause of many of these problems. Many times, we blame ourselves for our failed relationships in marriages, when, the majority of the time it is beyond our control, and we are innocent of the relationship failing.

Be encouraged look on the brighter side of things, if you know in your heart you were one hundred percent committed to the relationship before God as you promised in your vows, then you do not need to blame yourself or feel guilty, because you have done your best, that is what God requires of you is to do your best, and may be they were not the one for you after all, they did not deserve you. Looking back at all the pain and wounds of the past, will only let you hold unforgiveness and resentment, ask the Lord to give you strength to reverse this and use it in a positive way as a weapon to push you forward, to be a better person, an over comer to help yourself and others.

Remember you cannot change the past or change people's behavior, you are responsible for how you treat them in the eyes of God, but you can use this experience as a steppingstone to help others. And in turn you will help yourself and have peace and joy.

CHAPTER 19
HEALTHY HABITS AND LIFESTYLES FOR MARRIED COUPLES

As you both get older, your lifestyle changes, your body gets relaxed and slows down our metabolism decreases and we gain weight easily and eventually obesity set in and other health related issues, it is now in your lives if there is not a regular exercise regimen in place you
both need to start, check with your physician first to see if there is any major health issue that will cause any problems and let him or her give you the okay to start working out. exercise together is fun at least 3 to 4 times per week, for half an hour to an hour.

Remember as couples God wants you to live long, healthy and happy lives, God does not want you to die prematurely at an early age without completing your assignment here on earth.

There are many different activities you and your spouse can interact in together depending on your health, again consult your doctor before you start any exercise regimen. As couples working out together is much more fun and you motivate each other to continue, but if not do it for yourself, this is for your health and you living longer, here is a few simple exercises you can start with, such as walking, walking in different places or route will help to motivate you because it is like sightseeing, so it will not get boring quickly. Bike riding, golfing walk instead of using a golf cart, tennis, rocket ball, valley ball, baseball or soft ball, jogging, soccer, bowling, dancing, basketball, or join the gym, try and get into some type of activities as soon as possible. In addition, diet plays a very important part of keeping your health, you need to watch what you eat, the potion you eat, and also how late you eat, with these two combinations you will see a dramatic change in your health and how you feel. It will draw you closer as a married couple, it will make you more attractive to each other, and you both will be more active.

CHAPTER 20
SCRIPTURE REFERENCE FOR COUPLES

Scripture References: for couples during times of Praise and Worship
and during times of Trials and Togetherness in Marriages.

These are some scripture readings that may help during your times of needs

During Trials & Tribulations

2 Corinthians Chapter 8

Matthew 24 vs 21

John 16 vs 33

Romans 5 vs 3

Romans 12 vs 12

Romans 8

Job 14

Psalms 27

Psalms 46

1 Corinthians Chapter 7

Psalms 91

During Times of Thanksgiving

Luke 2 vs 38

Philippians 4 vs 6

1 Corinthians 15 vs 57

Ephesians 5 vs 6

During Times of Worship & Praise just because of who He is and what He is to you

Psalms 95 vs 6

Matthew 4 vs 9

John 4 Vs 20

Psalms 30 Vs 9

Psalms 42 vs 5

Psalms 63 vs 3

Psalms 145 vs 4

Proverbs 27 vs 21

Proverbs 31 vs 31

During Times of Study Together

Psalms 34

Amos 3 vs 3

Matthew 18 vs 20

Matthew 19 Vs 6

Romans 8 vs 28

1 Thessalonians 4 vs 17

Matthew 5 vs 32

Mark 12 vs 25

During Times of Individual Studies for Wives

Titus 2 vs 4

1 Corinthians 7

Proverbs 31

Ephesians 5

Luke 17

Proverbs 12

Proverbs 9

Proverbs 14

1 Timothy 2

1 Corinthians 13 vs 1-13

During Times of Individual Studies for Husbands

Proverbs 18 vs 22

Proverbs 19

Luke 14

Luke 17

Ephesians 5

1 Timothy 3

Proverbs 12

Matthew 5 vs 28

Proverbs 5 vs 18

1 Corinthians 7

1 Corinthians 13 vs 1-13

The Love Scripture

During times of individual studies and studies together when you feel as though you are falling out of love or falling apart and, or forgetting your vows

1 Corinthians 13 vs 1-13

Giving

Giving thanks during good or bad times as a couple, especially if you are a Christian couple, I urge you both not to give up on giving, Giving of your time is also a part of your offering it is not just monetarily, but also of yourselves to help build the church, the body of Christ.

As you both do your part and give of yourselves and time God will give you increase, he will show you areas of your lives that you never dreamed of, he will show you areas of your lives in ministry. kingdom work and your ministry will come forth, because you give of yourselves freely, He will close doors that need closing, and He will open doors that you did not know exist, some of these doors are starting your own business, new career or jobs changes, financial disasters, living from pay check to pay check, buying and owning your own home, wanting to be debt free, better health, better relationship with spouse and family.

Better health for your or loved ones, release of a loved ones in prison, praying for salvation for a loved one, friends and family to be saved. One of these doors that are critical in our lives as a couple is we pray for God to open is the financial doors, these financial doors will not open unless you are faithful, dedicated and committed giving your tithes 10% of your earnings, offerings is whatever you freely give is between you and God and your time back to God, this is not my words this is scriptures Malachi 3 vs 8-11. God wants you to know if you are committed and dedicated to him, in following what he asks you to do, He will be committed and dedicated to you in doing, what He promised He would do, it is a "covenant".

Many times as couples we start off well in doing good and as hard times comes we stop paying our tithes and pay bills, or we will give for a while and after wards we stop giving because we do not see it coming back immediately we stop giving, you need to understand and realize when you give sometimes it will come immediately and sometimes it takes time, remember it does not always come back in the form of money, but in other things we need. At times, we do not see any return for a while because God is testing our faithfulness.

As couples, many times in marital relationships husbands and wives have disagreements with finances especially when it comes to tithing. Out of everything you do as priority on your list, such as eating to live, paying your rent or mortgage to have a place to live, your tithes should be included in the prioritized order. If you do not do it the bible way you will always live under the level of prosperity that God wants for you. I want to encourage couples to communicate and agree to disagree on some priorities in your lives, especially your finances, ask yourselves these questions, are you happy financially with what you have in your savings account? are you happy with the income coming in? are you struggling financially? are you happy where you are financially? Do you need a change or to improve or increase your financial state? Some of these questions you may answer yes, some answers may be no. If you are one of these couples that need a drastic financial improvement, then you need to take an inventory of what, and how much you are giving to the Lord. Yet it seems so simple, it is simple, make sure the place you are giving your money is on good ground. If you are not giving at all or one spouse is giving, this is where your financial troubles lie, you will never have enough, it will always seem as if you are living beneath the privileges of how and where God wants you to live, prosperous lives. If one spouse continues to give, because of God covenant words, He will bless you because He is a "just God", but the blessing will not be complete to the fullest potential, of how He really wants to bless you, and this is because you are separated in your faith and giving so instead of being one you are two. So, to be blessed as a "whole" you must be in one accord together to be fully and completely blessed as one.

If you are not giving freely by murmuring, complaining, arguing, and grumbling, you will also stop your blessings. God wants you to give freely with a joyful heart, I challenge you to start giving faithfully with your time and money and live a fair and upright life and be a little patience and watch what God are about to do in your lives, you will never be the same, you will be in a state of shock and disbelief that whatever God his doing is happening to you.

When you give do not just fold or crush up your money like a piece of garbage or trash and toss it into the offering basket, each time you drop it, give it as if you are giving a gift to someone and then pray and ask God for what you want, give in expectation, He wants you to remind him of his words.

CHAPTER 21
MARRIED COUPLES IN AN UNEQUALLY YOKE RELATIONSHIP OR BACKSLIDING

To all my fellow Christian Brothers and Sisters, who have been cough up into an unequally yoke marriage or back sliding. I pray for you all that are praying for change and is holding on to your relationship, I also pray for your spouse too, those who are unsaved and or back sliding. I pray for God's persevering strength and patience for you to continue loving them.

Nothing is impossible with God. But it takes a lot of commitment, love and patience when you are into these relationships. Nothing is impossible but it will not be easy it takes a kind of person who is willing to have a "heart transplant" and a mindset of wanting to change, this is a goal that is reachable if you both work hard together if you want the relationship to work and continue in a positive direction, Two people with a spiritual mindset that is totally opposite, thoughts are different, lifestyle is different to a major extent, there actions and thinking is mostly worldly, while yours actions and thoughts are spiritually directed by the Lord. Nevertheless, you are now committed to keep your vows you both took in the sight of God, I do not know the reason you are in an unequally yoke marriage, may be it is because you were impatient to wait, and in the church there is more women than men and most are married and your hopes of finding a relationship was low or maybe you are an older person and you want to have a family before you get too old, or just may be your friends or family pushed you into it regardless of the circumstances and now you are married and you must make the best of the relationship.

Remember if you are the saved spouse in the home, keep in mind they are watching your every action and word, this will in turn cause the unsaved to decide either to turn their lives over to the Lord or continue living life as usual.

If your spouse does decide to give their lives to the Lord, then that is great and now you both can work together on one accord serving God and doing your best towards each other. And if not do your best by showing them love, remember you are not responsible for how they treat you, but you are responsible for how you treat them in the sight of

God. I cautioned you, if your unsaved or back sliding spouse is unreasonable and wants you to choose between God, or serving the Lord for them, do not do it, it is a trap, never choose man over God, when men leaves God will always be there for you, you must be strong and take a stand, men do not have a heaven or hell to put you in the choice is now yours, these are some decisions and choices you must make, there may be times in our lives when we must come to a decision either they walk away or you must walk away because of you believe and in whom you believe. I do pray they will turn their lives over to God, spouses continue to live a life so they can see and believe and desire to change.

Back Sliding

Back Sliding: Is the act of turning from God after being converted, Denouncing God, falling back into the world, falling back into sins and doing things that does not please God.

Sometimes in our Christian marriage relationships, one spouse will be overcome by problems, hard times or hardships and they let go of God's hands instead of holding on, and they fall back into the worlds, system of drugs, alcohol, sex, gambling and partying. Again, nothing is possible with God, He can pull anyone through who seeks and needs help! in times of difficulties.

Spouses continue in prayers, patience, commitment and love towards them I believe with the help of God he will pull them through. If this spouse has a made-up mind to run after the things of this world and rejects God and does not want to rededicate or recommit their lives, then you as the save spouse need to continue in the things of God, do not let them pull you into a back-sliding position, back into the world, it is not worth it.

CHAPTER 22
TURNING YOUR HOUSE INTO A HOME

As married couples, we are all guilty of not turning our house into homes! no need to point fingers, the time is now! we are in critical times as Christian married couples, we need to keep it together, the enemy is fighting harder than ever before any union that is ordained of God and he is at our heels constantly. As you have already known the divorce rate has skyrocket to 70% and we as Christians are included into that number, as the secular world is watching us thinking we should and is holding it together.

To be honest most of them are holding it together better than us, something is wrong with this picture! I can urge you to continue in prayer for change for yourself and your spouse, communication, compromise, listening, not just to hear and pay close attention to each other's needs and feelings. Do all that is possible to keep it together, do your best, again communication is key in keeping the relationship alive, if there is no communication there is no marriage. I know you are probably asking this question, what do I mean by tuning a house into a home, it is simple, we all know the enemy is working overtime to destroy our relationships, we are being perused continually without end, tearing us and each other apart, and tearing us down causing separation, conflict and strife.

We also know some work in the secular world and some of us are fortunate to own our own businesses but regardless we still must work or do business within the secular arena, and at times doing business with some Christians and or businesses and they are sometimes worse than

the secular ones, so we are daily fighting off the enemy as we go through our trials and tribulations.

Some of the flaws are ours, because when we leave the offices and our jobs instead of leaving the jobs behind, we take them home with us. We must transform our minds once we leave our jobs or businesses and know that home is home and no matter what went on at the job either good or bad that must be left behind when you go home to your family, you must be that husband or wife, father or mother when you come into the atmosphere of home. A home-like atmosphere is one where you should always look forward towards the end of the day to come home to casting all the cares of the office duties behind.

This is the kind of atmosphere you look forward to kicking back and relaxing, pulling your hair down, put your feet up in total relaxation. For couples who

both work meal preparation should be worked out who is the better cook or who is cooking this week or who reaches home first start cooking or if you can't cook bring something home or you if you both agree on eating out once or twice per week or if it is a special occasion, regardless of

if you dine in or out you want to come home to a relaxing atmosphere, preferably with soft relaxing music and later in the evening relax to some type of romance movie will bring in the mood for the rest of the evening.

If one or both people work outside the home, try and look decent and presentable to your husband or your wife when they come home even if you are tired, you want to keep the attraction. I am stressing again the importance of being presentable as I stated in the previous chapters, you should make your spouse felt welcome and special. This is for the sisters who like to walk around all day in tonight caps and scarf and rollers in your hair and house coats and dresses as if this is the only and favorite outfit you own, there is nothing wrong if this is what you like, but you should change and be presentable for your husband when he comes home.

Brothers, I am also talking to you, if you stay home and have a favorite outfit that you wear repeatedly just because it is comfortable as if that's the only one you own you also need to change and be presentable for your wife, I know they do not love you for what you wear, but it is good to change in to something different sometimes.

It is a turn on to your spouse, it keeps the relationship fresh, and spicy up your marriage, with small things like these among other things. Also, I do not care how bad things get your wife should not have to remind you to go and get a haircut. This goes for the wives too, he should not have

to tell you to go get your hair done, keep yourself up. As the cliché goes "A man's home is his castle". If a person can't go home and be happy and have peace, then what's the sense!

Keeping Your Dog on A Leash

My Pastor once preached a message about "Keeping Your Dog on A Leash" and I believe this message was an eye opener for married couples and singles who are involved in any relationship leading into marriage, this message may sound funny, but it is true. He was talking on how after a while in marriages, some wives and husbands become lackadaisical and start taking their spouses for granted, just because they are there and they believe they can treat them any way they want especially if they have been together for long period of time, so they put on the " old rusty leash" on their necks to keep them there as if they are dogs and they feed them when they want, and how they want to by tossing a plate of food to them and give them love once in a while by rubbing and bathing them and because they have been together for so long they take for granted they will just be satisfied with whatever they are giving them, and one day if not careful a "stray dogs" come a long and lick his or her face, rub his or her head and a bath them more often than usual and this is the kind of treatment they have been starving for, so one day when they had enough and break free from the "rusty leash" they will head where they feel loved.

So, the meaning of the story is this, do not take your spouses for granted just because you have been together for a long time, thinking they will stay and will not get tired and decided to leave and walk away from the relationship, because even a dog want to be loved. If you are not treating your husband or wife with love, kindness and respect, and you are taking them for granted you need to stop it. Change your attitude and selfish behaviors towards them, you should treat them the way you wanted to be treated, be humble towards each other, make and spend that quality

time. If you have been married for a long time and do not know what to do anymore ask God to direct, you so you can do and see things differently.

But always make your home warm and welcoming as they come home, greet them and tell them how much you miss, love and appreciate them. Pay close attention to their needs, do not let your spouse beg for your attention, and Affection, Do not deprive them of your love. The scripture says "Let the Husband render unto the wife due benevolence "and likewise, also the wife unto the husbands. The wife hath not power over her own body, but the husband: and likewise, also the husband hath not power of his own body, but the wife. Defraud ye not one the other, except it be with consent for a time, that ye may give yourselves to fasting and prayer; and come together again, that Satan tempt you not for your incontinency ".

Again, do not take them for granted, just because you see them every day. As you can see the enemy is not playing for keeps, he is playing to kill, steal and destroy your relationship, do not leave it unprotected.

CHAPTER 23
COUPLES CELEBRATING SPECIAL OCCASIONS

As married couples, celebrating special occasions should not be a one-sided event. What I mean by this is this, as a couple you are now one, it is no longer be "Me. My. and I" It should be ours, except for one or two special occasions out of the year that only one person can celebrate, such as birthdays. Occasions such as your anniversaries and valentine's day or any occasions both of you should be participate in, if it involved some type of gift exchange, again it should not be one sided where only one person is giving or exchanging gifts, you are both celebrations that special

occasion together and it should be shared. Just like your marriage, it is two people involved.

You should be thoughtful and considerate towards each other, remember, it is the thought that counts. How would you feel if on one of these special occasions that is supposed to be special for both of you, you were always the only person giving! you would feel used or feel as if you are being taken for granted? and after a while, deep inside resentment starts to build up. This is what the enemy uses to start a breakdown in the relationship, especially if there is no communication.

In the event, someone blesses you out of the "blue" and gives you a monetary gift and you know your spouse does not have any funds, I believe you should not be selfish and share it with your spouse. I do not believe you should be saying "this is mine ", and they blessed me with this, and I am keeping it all for myself, with this kind of behavior and mind set, this is the reason some many marriages fall apart.

As we already know, the husbands should be the head of the households, if he is a good provider, a hard worker, and he takes care of business and he sacrifices for the family, there should not be any hiding of anything. If the woman is presently the bread winner or the head of the household, she should help him to cover these bills or expenses until he is able to find employment, things happen, it is life, we should be each other's helpmate. I observed some married couples, on such occasions such as valentine's day and I see's the female spouses just waiting with their hands out for a gift from their husbands or whomever they are courting waiting to be wine and dine with chocolate, flowers, or whatever it may be, the male is the one usually is giving and the female is usually receiving and is not giving back much. Maybe I am misunderstanding this concept, but it should go both ways. I believe if you treat him like a "king" he will in turn treat you like a "queen" unless they just do not appreciate what God has given them, and if this is the issue then eventually when they get tired and they are gone this is usually the time they realize what they had when it's too late. So again, I encourage you to be thoughtful towards each other, be kind, unselfish, and love each other, do not take each other for granted, life is too short "we are here today and gone tomorrow", tomorrow is not promised to no man so please treat each other with kindness, take good care of each other, I cautioned you to do so, in the case God decide to take one of you home there should be no regrets.

CHAPTER 24
SEXUAL MANIPULATION IN MARRIAGES

As I look and listen to what is going on around and about me in this world, I learn both by experience and what I see and hear other's doing and experiencing. As children of God and believers following Christ, I left off from living and behaving like the world. I believe we should not be manipulators of our spouses, when it comes to "love making" I am referring to both men and women when it comes to the bedroom, especially when women talk of "holding sex" from their husbands until they get what they want or holding sex from them because they make them angry or just "holding out" on each other until they feel like it. My dear sisters and brothers, you may be upset at me while reading this, it may strike a chord, the truth is being revealed, to you, but I am so sorry it hurts you, but the truth shall set you free. I must write as the Holy Spirit directs me to write, each individual must take an inventory of their own lives and behaviors, and will and must answer to God, this is one of the reasons we make our "vows" That is why the scriptures states "marriage is honorable in all and the bed is undefiled".

As long as you are married to each other, God is happy whatever you do to each other and for each other to make yourselves happy. Do not continue to manipulate each other and was each other as targets to get what you want, if you sit and think about it, it is just a trick from the enemy to cause conflicts in your relationship sooner or later. You as women must remember, men are weak, I am speaking of human beings in general, and yes, there are some men and women that is weak in this area, no matter how long they have been saved or how "controlled" they are, people have weaknesses and sometimes falls prey to temptation. So, I plead with both men and women, do not continue in these behaviors towards each other, eventually it will only harm you and your relationship take it seriously.

We do not need any more statistics into the resolution of our Christian marriages while the devil sits on the sideline and laugh. We all know that this is one of his old tricks and it still works, and is still effective, it is called "deceit", and you are deceiving, hurting each other by giving him the ammunition to use you. And you are ripping your children and family apart.

Let me address this issue, it is very critical if your relationship is to continue, most women cause a detrimental to their marriage, some women thinks once they are in a marriage as time passes by they do not need to continue "caring for their spouse sexual needs" and satisfy them, some does not care how they carry themselves anymore, some ignore their spouse the longer they are in the relationship. They are not thinking or being aware that there are "vultures" or the "clean up woman" just waiting in the shadows to entice him and clean up what she does not want to do as a wife, therefore making their relationship vulnerable to others, by refusing to full fill his needs, rejecting him, and pushing him away.

A man can only take so much, his manhood and pride will be seared and believe me the "vultures" and "clean up woman" is watching just waiting to entice him into her trap because he is weak. So Sisters , please do your duty, be wise, you know sexual relations is a vital part of the marriage relationship, ladies be realistic and honest with yourselves, think about if it was your sexual needs and he his "holding out" on you, how would you feel? think about the hurt and rejection you would feel, you would feel like you are less than a woman and you would wonder if he is looking else wear. This is one of the "primary" reasons men go out on their wives. You do not want this in your relationship. Do the right thing, do not let him "stray" and run into someone else arms, again if something is wrong physically go and seek professional medical help, and do not let him "burn".

CHAPTER 25
SEXUAL MANIPULATION IN MARRIAGES

This is life, we are living in a real world, the enemy is angry and does not want to see us happy, and walking and working together, so the world could be drawn and want what we have. But regardless of the conflicts, disagreements, misunderstandings, miscommunication, or lack of communication, these are simple issues that can be resolved and not get blown out of proportion and escalate. But sometimes because of our foolish pride, disobedience, stubbornness or just plain selfishness it will not let us accept reality of the simple facts that we need to take time out sit down and talk resolved these issues before they become too large to put under control.

Simply Taking Time Out to Talk With Each Other

Take some time out to talk with each other, find a convenient time that is good for both of you if you are unable to talk face to face write it down your thoughts on paper, things that are bothering you. Do not try and bombard each other after work, this is not a good time to give him or her time to rest and relax before starting your talk. Sometimes we tend to take for granted words we express to each other, it goes through one ear and come through the next, writing things on paper tend to catch their attention of our spouses, because it seems more urgent when it is written to take into consideration.

Anger

Unfortunately, this is part of life's reality, we will get angry each other sometimes, we just cannot pretend that we will never go through periods of anger in our relationships, as long as you do not stay there, even the bible states, that it is okay to be angry but sin not, but not to let the

sun goes down on your wrath, meaning to resolve the issue before you go to sleep. It will not always be peaches and cream, but if you need to take "time out" to calm down, walk away if you must.

Many times, a peaceful and tranquil walk will help to relax your mind, it will make you see things differently, it sometimes reveal you might be the one at fault, took things wrong and blow it out of proportion, and after you return home if you are honest enough with yourself and God, you will simply ask for forgiveness and ask the Lord to bring peace into your home and how to approach and resolved the issues. If one spouse is still angry and the other is calm, leave it alone until both of you are completely calm and is able to talk respectfully with each other.

Unresolved Disagreements

If you Both have unresolved disagreements, that there is just no way you both can resolved the issues, and it is too painful or hard to talk with one another about the issues at hand or you both are still angry at each other and there is unforgiveness and disrespect towards each other, first ask the Lord for forgiveness and forgive yourself. At this point it would be wise to seek out professional counseling help.

CHAPTER 26
AUTHORITY FIGURE IN YOUR MARRIAGE

Men, as husbands God has made and called you to be the authority figure in your home and marriages. He made you to be "ruler and head" of your household.

First, He made you to be that "Priest, Prophet and King" over everything. also, set you as leader to be responsible for everything he placed you over.

He also gives you headship as provider over everything he placed in your hands. As a Protector and a husband God made you to be in charge, so this made you the L.5P.K, this stands for the following.

A Leader: is one who leads, directing or commanding and guiding a head or put to dominate over the house and other responsibilities He places in your hand.

A Provider: is one who provides for himself and his family, whether it may be food, shelter, clothing, education and give love.

A Proctor: is a person that protects or is a guardian and a defender of his family and home.

A Priest: is one who goes to the Lord on the behalf of others and delegates, runs those orders to lead his home and his family.

A Prophet: is one who under the divine inspiration of God hears, give answers, delegates and guides, directs and leads his businesses, family into the present and future events of their lives.

A King: A male ruler, who rules or run his kingdom or domain, this his home, family, business affairs, this is a man who is highly successful and takes responsibility and authority.

Words to The Wives

Ladies, you know God have blessed you with good husbands, please be that wife God called you to be, be there at their sides be that helpmate, be that praying woman and cover him daily, if you do not know what to pray for, pray in the spirit, your husbands are under pressure as the head and as leaders as men of God. Do not add additional stress on him, do not be that nagging wife.

CHAPTER 27
PRIDE DISRESPECT AND ABUSE IN MARRIAGES

Disrespect and abuse, weather it is physical or verbal, can either come from the male or the female or both in a relationship, regardless of who it comes from, God is displeased.

Because He gave us each other for companionship and as a help mate. He gave us each other to love, cherish and to care for each other. We as Christian should be an example to the "world", instead most of our marriages are failing and some of the secular marriages are lasting much longer than most of our Christian ones. The divorce rate is about equal to the world. When it comes to disrespect in a relationship, one or each spouse loses the respect for each other they once had for each other, then a breakdown of the relationship starts slowly if not corrected and then the marriage slowly determinates, then they lose their love, then a slow increase in arguing is pronounced, then a decreasing in the time spending together, and additional responsibilities in the relationship. I notice sometimes how some wives or husbands speak to or answer their spouses in public, it is shameful and embarrassing, it should not be so. If there is anger towards each other, there still should be respect and self-control until you both get behind closed doors, with this being so, do not leave the doors open for the enemy to creep in or other people observing and gossiping.

Many times, this disrespect comes from people 's pride.

Pride is where one spouse feels like they are outgrowing their spouses, especially in the ministry, one spouse is may be reaching higher in their calling, destiny or calling they were created to walking, now that they are walking into their purpose and their spouse is not yet walking theirs and it becomes a problem because they feel as if they have "arrived" and now they want to rule the world and everybody around them and talk to them any way they want. Spouses need to realize when you speak to each other, it is not what you say, but how you say it, it is the "tone of voice "you use when you talk and your body language or facial expression. If they start to make better salaries, some feels as if they are better than their spouses, some forget that these "gifts" comes from God, and it is for his purpose and glory not theirs. God wants you to honor your marriage and your spouse's regardless of your "title" He wants you to love, respect and care for each other it is a covenant. If it comes to a point where you need outside help, then go ahead and get it, if it means saving your marriage go and get the help you need, put away your foolish pride and do not worry about others knowing you are having problems. this is the reason the Lord made counselors with experience and wisdom to help us in times of need.

Pride in Marriages

Pride is one of the most harmful behaviors in a marriage relationship, this is when one or both spouses fail to put their prideful behaviors aside and communicate or compromise and say I am sorry when they are at wrong. Pride will cause separation and divorce and when it comes to fruition, it only causes regrets, sorrow, and hurting while the devil sits aside and laughs while you are in misery.

CHAPTER 28
TO THE WIDOWS AND THE WIDOWERS

To all the singles that are widows and widowers first my condolences go out to you, whether it was yesterday or ten years ago. A loss of a Beloved spouse is very heard, and it takes time to heal, some takes longer than others and some never gets over it depending on the circumstances, but regardless of the loss it will remain in our hearts especially if it was a remarkable person. Some may choose to go on in life and start over into a new relationships, while others may continue to be widowers and widows, if you made that decision to live your life as a single there is nothing wrong with that it is healthy as long as you are not doing it because of guilt, and you felt as though they were good to you and was married for a long time and now you feel as though you are betraying them. If you chose to love again and start dating or courting, I cautioned you to give yourself some time to heal. Take your time in the dating process to see who is. I know after being in a relation for a long time after a loss you will tend to get lonely and want companionship but be very careful you don't want to rush into any relationships because you are lonely or desperate to have someone, this could prove to be dangerous and hear breaking as time goes by.

Everyone wants someone to love and for that love to be returned. Again, seek someone who is compatible with you and shares the same similarities as you. And if some called themselves Christians and you are a child of God make sure you are patient and ask for discernment to see who they are what they are after, their motives, because there are some out there that pray on the innocent, they called them "wolves in sheep's clothing". so, beware and very careful guard your hearts, you are already vulnerable and are already hurting from your loss you don't need someone to come into your life and hurt you again, Most of these wolves knows you are lonely and are seeking companionship, so they specifically pray for people like you because they believed you are probably established and are financially secured.

CHAPTER 29
CONTIUING THE ROMANCE

If it is your first year or your sixtieth year in marriage, the same techniques you used to capture their heart during courting or dating, is the same technique you need to keep their attention and spice in the marriage to keep it going. Just because the courtship or dating ends you both must now keep the marriage on going as if you were still courting.

Four Things Is A Must In Your Marriage For It To Last

The first is **Severance**; is separating yourself by prioritizing relationships between your parents, children, and family in order for your marriage to work. You must restructure your relationship, you must sever yourself and them from you to a certain extent, the scripture says; Therefore, shall a man leave his father, and mother, and shall cleave unto his wife: and they shall be one flesh. Genesis 2 verses 24.

The next is **Permanence;** is staying power in a relationship, it is reassurance that we are in this marriage for ever until death do us part, through thick or thin, good or bad, in sickness or in health.

The next is **Unity;** is coming together on one accord, Unity is when we sacrifice and lay aside our own needs and desires for our spouses, it is self-sacrifice, it is not only what you want but also what your spouse wants.

The next is **Intimacy;** Intimacy is not only love making, but it is the ability to be transparent with yourself and with each other, you should be able to be yourself around your husband or wife, you should be able to be "naked" and not a shame and should be able to share anything with your spouse without it being thrown in your face when there are disagreements, and anger.

Appendix

Bible: King James Version 2003

Dictionary: Webster's 1988

A Little About the Author.

Ms. Angela C. Griffiths has been a Christian for several years. She lives in the City of Orland, Florida, she is a member of a local church, has one daughter. This is her first book and is presently writing others inspirational books. In 2006 After the passing of her beloved mother she received a prophetic word, that she has the gift of writing and will be writing, three years later she received a second prophetic word of confirmation that opened her eyes that the Lord was serious, so she decided to surrender herself to him to be used in whatever area's He sees fit for his use.

Made in United States
Orlando, FL
27 December 2024